Quarterly Essay

CONTENTS

I0038946

Quarterly Essay is published four times a year by Black Inc., an imprint of Schwartz Media Pty Ltd. Publisher: Morry Schwartz.

ISBN 978-1-86395-488-4 ISSN 1832-0953

Subscriptions – 1 year (4 issues): $49 within Australia incl. GST. Outside Australia $79.
2 years (8 issues): $95 within Australia incl. GST. Outside Australia $155.

Payment may be made by Mastercard or Visa, or by cheque made out to Schwartz Media. Payment includes postage and handling.

To subscribe, fill out and post the subscription card or form inside this issue, or subscribe online:

www.quarterlyessay.com
subscribe@blackincbooks.com
Phone: 61 3 9486 0288

Correspondence should be addressed to:

The Editor, Quarterly Essay
37–39 Langridge Street
Collingwood VIC 3066 Australia
Phone: 61 3 9486 0288 / Fax: 61 3 9486 0244
Email: quarterlyessay@blackincbooks.com

Editor: Chris Feik. Management: Sophy Williams, Caitlin Yates. Publicity: Elisabeth Young. Design: Guy Mirabella. Assistant Editor: Adam Shaw. Typesetting: Duncan Blachford

POWER
SHIFT

Australia's Future between
Washington and Beijing

Hugh White

There is a problem with Australia's vision of its future. On the one hand, we assume that China will just keep growing indefinitely, buying more and more from our miners at higher and higher prices. On the other hand, we expect America to remain the strongest power in Asia, the region's natural leader and Australia's ultimate protector. We will have a very nice future if both these things happen. The problem is that they cannot both happen at once. If China grows fast enough to keep our economy buoyant, it will overtake America to become the richest country in the world sometime around 2030. That will make it too strong to live under American leadership in Asia. It will look to lead in its own right, and challenge America's position.

Asia will be transformed by what follows, and so will Australia. For forty years America's dominant place in Asia has been essentially uncontested by China and the region's other strong states. That has kept Asia remarkably peaceful and made Australia very secure. China's growing wealth and power, by contesting America's leadership, upsets all this. A new order will appear in Asia, which may not be as peaceful and stable as the one that has served us so well for over a generation. Australia will find itself in a different and perhaps more dangerous region, facing higher risks of conflict and fewer economic opportunities. We could easily end up both poorer and less secure than we are today.

The foundations of Asia's political and strategic order are already shifting. This year China overtook Japan to become the world's second-biggest economy. It is already bigger, relative to the US, than the Soviet Union ever was during the Cold War. A Chinese challenge to American power in Asia is no longer a future possibility but a current reality. Few issues are more important to Australia's future than how this plays out. You would not know it to listen to our leaders. Even Kevin Rudd, who understands Asia's dynamics as well as anyone, avoided the issue as prime minister, worried that it might make voters uneasy. Tony Abbott dismissed the whole question when he wrote in his book *Battlelines* that by 2020, "The United States will still have the world's strongest economy by far" and China's rise "may not mean much change for Australia's international relationships or foreign policy priorities." Julia Gillard seems never to have thought about it at all.

Our leaders, and by extension the rest of us, are assuming that Asia will be transformed economically over the next few decades, but remain unchanged strategically and politically. It is an appealing assumption because the past forty years have been among the best times in Australia's history, and it has been easy to believe that American power would continue indefinitely to keep Asia peaceful and Australia safe. That has been a cardinal mistake. To see why, we need to know what made the last few decades so good.

*

For one hundred years – roughly from 1870 to 1970 – Asia was convulsed by the power politics of strong states. Russia, Britain, France, Germany, Japan and America all jostled for markets and political influence. This made them strategic competitors and led to many big wars, culminating in the Pacific War that ended at Hiroshima and Nagasaki. After 1945 the power politics continued, as Asia became a theatre of the Cold War. Then, in the early 1970s, the power politics virtually stopped. Since then, relations among Asia's strongest states have been remarkably harmonious. Armed force has played little or no role; fear of one another has not driven their defence planning. They have not tried to attract client states and build spheres of influence against one another, nor have they set out to subvert one another's internal politics or nobble one another's economies. Above all, they have kept the peace. Aside from a few minor skirmishes, no major Asian power has been involved in substantial military operations in East Asia since China "taught Vietnam a lesson" in 1979. It is probably the longest period of peace in Asia's long history, and certainly a big change from the previous century.

Why did this happen? One argument is that closer economic integration has fundamentally transformed the way countries relate to one another. In a globalised world, trade, investment and other forms of interaction are so important that governments cannot afford to disrupt them, so old-style power politics has disappeared because it doesn't pay. This may be part of the explanation, but it cannot be the whole story, and it is probably not the most important part. Asia's stable order has been as much a cause as a result of economic integration and growth, because the great powers had to stop competing strategically before Asia's economic integration could get going. So what started the virtuous cycle of stability and growth in the first place?

No one expected that things would work out so well when Asia's era of peace began almost forty years ago. The late 1960s and early 1970s was a time of great uncertainty. China was seen as a rising power, Japan chafed at the constraints of its post-war settlement, the Soviets were looking elsewhere, India loomed unpredictably, and America seemed weakened and demoralised by failure in Vietnam. It seemed that Asia was headed for an even more dangerous era than the preceding few decades, with a new, more equal, more fluid and more unstable balance of power among all these strong states.

But that did not happen. Instead, America emerged from failure in Vietnam stronger in Asia than ever, because for the first time its position became uncontested by Asia's two next-strongest countries, Japan and China. This was not just an accident of history, but the result of a remarkable piece of strategic diplomacy by two of the most ambiguous characters in recent history: Richard Nixon and Henry Kissinger. Nixon, advised by Kissinger, went to Beijing in 1972 and cut a deal with Mao. America would stop pretending that the nationalist regime in Taiwan was the government of China and recognise instead the communist government in Beijing. In return, China would stop contesting America's position in Asia and stop supporting communist insurgencies around the region.

Today the deal sounds merely sensible, but at the time it required real vision and courage from each side. Both had to give up a lot, but both had a lot to gain. For America, recognising the communists in Beijing was a huge concession, which only a hard-right Republican like Nixon could have sold politically. But Nixon knew the only way to get out of Vietnam was to end the strategic competition with China, which had dragged America into the war in the first place; furthermore, winning the support of China against the Soviets would help turn the tide in the Cold War. Beijing had to relinquish its ambitions to build an empire of communist satellites in Asia and tone down two decades of anti-US rhetoric. In return, China got protection against the Soviet Union, insurance against the risk of a resurgent Japan, breathing space to deal with chaos at home, and the opportunity to open China economically to the West.

And so the deal was done. Then Japan was brought in; Tokyo had to be persuaded to remain America's strategic client and accept America's new relationship with China. In return, it got continued protection against the Soviets, and against China as well. The deal carried real strategic and political costs for Japan, but also delivered huge benefits, as Japan's economy enjoyed another twenty years of remarkable growth. Asia's middle and smaller powers benefited too. When the major powers stopped competing with one another, they stopped interfering in the affairs of smaller countries. Left to themselves, the Southeast Asians flourished economically and developed politically, and they built a strong regional connection in the Association of Southeast Asian Nations (ASEAN), eventually bringing the war-ravaged countries of Indochina into the fold.

For almost forty years, then, Asia's strategic stability, political evolution, regional integration and economic growth have all been underwritten by the deals struck by China and Japan to accept American leadership. No country has done better out of this than Australia. Politically we have been able to enmesh ourselves in Asia while staying close to America, because America has been welcomed throughout Asia. The stability has underpinned Australia's growth by allowing Asia's manufacturing giants, and therefore our exports, to boom. Uncontested American primacy has kept the risk of major conflict in Asia very low. Australia has faced no calls to support America against major military threats in Asia, and we have faced none of our own. That has kept our defence needs modest and our defence budget low. No wonder we would like things to stay the same.

If sustained, China's rise marks the end of the post-Vietnam War era. Yet it may mean even more than that: it may mark the passing of the epoch of Western dominance in Asia that began five centuries ago, in 1498, when Vasco da Gama brought Portuguese naval power to India. America's role today is simply the latest episode of what scholars call the Vasco da Gama epoch. It could also be the last. If China successfully contests American primacy over the next few decades, Western power will no longer hold strategic sway and Asia will be master of its own affairs once more.

The prospect is momentous for everyone in Asia, but especially for Australia, because our country owes its very existence to the Vasco da Gama epoch in its later, Anglo-Saxon, phases. Ever since Australia was founded in 1788, the domination of Asia's oceans by Britain, and later by America, has seemed both necessary and sufficient for our security. Nurturing alliances with these powers and supporting their primacy in Asia have been the permanent central pillars of Australian foreign policy since we first started to think about our place in the world. If China's power displaces America's primacy, we will have to start thinking about our place in the world all over again from the ground up, and make choices we have never before faced.

We have seen this coming for a while. As long ago as the early 1990s, the end of the Cold War and the Soviet collapse, as well as China's economic trajectory, suggested that Asia was in for big changes. Both Bob Hawke and Paul Keating began to explore what this might mean for Australia and how we should respond. Both men knew how important American leadership was to Asia, and saw a risk that, suffering economically, it might disengage as the Soviet threat disappeared. They promoted Asia-Pacific Economic Cooperation (APEC) as a forum to counteract that trend and to help hold America in Asia. Both also saw the immense economic promise of China and worked hard to capitalise on it. And they saw that however much we maintained the alliance with America, a new level of engagement in Asia's affairs was going to be essential for Australia. They both spoke of Australia needing to look for security "in Asia, not from Asia."

By the time John Howard became prime minister in 1996, the picture had changed. Many people – not just Americans – believed that America had become economically, militarily and ideologically unchallengeable. Fears that the US might disengage from Asia disappeared, replaced by visions of a new era of American unipolarity in which it would exercise uncontested predominance for as far ahead as could be seen, not just in Asia but around the world. Yet at the same time, the scale and momentum of China's rise started to sink in. As the trauma of the Tiananmen Square crisis faded, and Japan's problems deepened, it became clear to everyone that China was the big story of Asia. Howard was not expecting this when he took office. "How long has this been going on?" he asked, gazing at Shanghai's ever-rising skyline from his hotel window on his first visit there as prime minister in April 1997. Yet he quickly grasped what it could mean for Australia and was determined to do whatever it took to increase trade between the two countries.

Just as quickly he realised that the new era would complicate Australia's foreign policy. A few weeks after winning office in early 1996, Howard had instinctively backed Washington all the way against China in a crisis over Taiwan. Beijing hit back, putting the relationship with Canberra in the deep freeze for months. Howard learned the lesson: building trade with China required greater respect for China's wishes, which in turn required adjustments to other parts of Australia's international posture – even when it came to the US alliance itself. From then on, he went quite a long way to meet Beijing's expectations.

Just how far became clear in October 2003, when a coincidence of scheduling found George W. Bush and Hu Jintao visiting Canberra on consecutive days. Like previous US presidents, Bush was invited to address the parliament, but Howard also extended the same invitation to Hu. This produced the rather surreal spectacle of Canberra's political classes filing into the chamber to hear Bush on one day, and Hu the next. It also conveyed an impression of parity in Australia's two most important relationships, especially as Hu was the first foreign leader other than a US president ever to be invited to address the Australian parliament.

That impression became clearer still when Howard rose to welcome President Hu. He acknowledged how fast the relationship with China was changing when he said that ten years before, an occasion such as this would have been "highly improbable." And then, speaking of the importance of the US–China relationship to Australia, he said:

> Our aim is to see calm and constructive dialogue between the United States and China on those issues which might potentially cause tension between them. It will be Australia's aim, as a nation which has different but nonetheless close relationships with both of those nations, to promote that constructive and calm dialogue.

It was a remarkable statement coming from a man of Howard's political disposition: he was describing Australia as equidistant from the US and China, and neutral between them – a kind of go-between. The impression was amplified the following year in Beijing when Howard's foreign minister, Alexander Downer, proclaimed that Australia now had not just an economic relationship with Beijing, but also a strategic and political partnership. Challenged by the journalist Hamish McDonald to explain how that strategic partnership would fare if America and China went to war over Taiwan, Downer replied that there would be no problem: the ANZUS Treaty would not require Australia to support the US in such a war because it fell outside the treaty's geographical scope. This came as news to Washington; diplomats squawked and Downer backtracked a few days later. Nonetheless, the message had been sent: America could no longer rely on Australia's automatic support in disputes with China, even on issues as fundamental as Taiwan. China was becoming too important to us.

The shift towards China was obscured by Howard's strong support for Bush after 9/11, especially on Iraq. Yet Howard accepted China's growing leadership role in Asia, declined to criticise its military build-up, sought eagerly to join the East Asia Summit (EAS) without US involvement and, until his last year in office, steered clear of American and Japanese efforts to draw Australia into a coalition of democracies designed to resist the Chinese challenge to American primacy.

At the same time, Howard's Defence White Paper, released in 2000, clearly acknowledged that China's rise constituted a major change in Australia's circumstances, and that Australia needed to take a wider view of its national interests and expand its military capabilities. The possibility of war with China now influenced major force-planning decisions for the first time since the Vietnam War.

Howard never really explained all of this to the Australian public. While steadily sliding China's way, he assured Australians that they did not have to choose between the US and China, saying that escalating rivalry between them was not "inevitable" – which was true but evasive. As so often with Howard, it is unclear to what extent these evasions were conscious and deliberate.

There was much less ambiguity about Kevin Rudd. He came to the Lodge with a deep understanding of China's trajectory and its implications for Australia, and at times he spoke about the matter quite frankly. In launching his ill-fated Asia-Pacific Community concept in 2008, Rudd noted that the rise of China would fundamentally change Asia and spoke of the need to design a new order. In September 2008, in a speech setting the scene for the release of the 2009 Defence White Paper, Rudd predicted that China could overtake the US to become the largest economy in the world as early as 2020, and suggested that China's growing power could threaten Australia.

The 2009 White Paper picked up these themes, but it also said that America would remain the strongest power in Asia for as far ahead as we could see. It foreshadowed major expansions of Australia's naval forces in the 2040s and beyond, but implied that for the next few decades Australia could assume that nothing would change. Rudd's messages were therefore very mixed: yes, China's rise changes Asia's strategic order fundamentally; but no, America will remain in charge and Australia faces no increased risk for many years, if ever. In the end, while Rudd understood China's rise better than Howard, he was just as unwilling to explain to Australians what it meant. There is no reason to expect that the present generation of political leaders will do any better.

Like climate change, the issue seems too hard for our political system to handle. Despite the clear trends, it is simply too difficult for us to conceive that Australia might no longer be able to rely for protection on the world's richest and strongest country. And it is easy to hope that, like climate change, the issue will just go away.

CHINA CATCHES UP

Why should China's rise disrupt the Asian order when stability is so obviously in everyone's interests? The answer goes back to the original deal that settled regional relationships in 1972. The deal was built on the relative power of the three key countries at the time: the US, China and Japan. Since then, many things have changed. The Soviet Union has disappeared, Japan has grown and then stagnated, India has emerged as a major Asian power, and China has taken off. Inevitably, the further these developments shift the power balance from the way it was in 1972, the shakier the foundations of the deal become. Of these shifts, the most important today is China's.

We therefore need to take a closer look at China, the better to understand its growth and what follows from it. We will do this from the long-term perspective of power politics, which deals in decades rather than quarterly accounting periods. China is inherently a rich, strong country. Throughout history it has usually had the world's largest GDP, simply because it has had the most people. The arithmetic is simple: as long as workers everywhere produce roughly the same amount, the country with the biggest workforce has the biggest economy. This arithmetic only stopped working in China's favour around the time Australia was founded. Until the mid-eighteenth century Britain's workers were not much more productive than China's, but the Industrial Revolution transformed the way people worked and how much they produced. Per-capita output took off and by the 1820s, 20 million Britons produced more than 380 million Chinese did, and Britain overtook China to become the wealthiest country in the world. No longer did the biggest population mean the biggest economy.

The Industrial Revolution broke the nexus between population and power for two centuries, and because it spread unevenly, it did a lot to shape the world of today. From Britain it moved quickly to Europe and the United States. After 1854 it flourished in Japan, and in the late nineteenth century it started to take hold in Russia. These countries gained a huge advantage over the rest. The Europeans became strong enough to colonise much of the globe. Britain's early lead meant that it remained the world's largest economy until about 1880, when America took over. Again, the simple arithmetic of national output was at work: American workers had become as productive as Britain's, and thanks to massive immigration there were more of them. America became the largest economy in the world simply because it had the largest workforce to achieve and sustain industrial levels of output per worker. That has been true ever since.

China missed out and paid a terrible price. Europeans had been trading in Asia since 1500, but they hardly touched China until the Industrial Revolution, which increased both their power and their appetite. Led by the British, they forced their way into China, undermining its government and eroding its sovereignty. Many Chinese realised that to compete with the West, China must remake itself as a modern state with a modern, high-productivity economy. It took them more than a century. Early upheavals like the Boxer Rebellion led to the revolution of 1911 and the establishment of a republic. Another forty years of chaos and invasion passed before a strong, unified central government at last re-established effective control over the country under the Chinese Communist Party.

Unfortunately, the party imposed unstable, faction-ridden politics under Mao's erratic leadership, counter-productive foreign policies and a totally dysfunctional economic philosophy. It took another thirty years to remedy these defects. In 1972, China accepted the reality of US power and began to work with America to stabilise Asia's regional order. After Mao died in 1976, the Communist Party slowly evolved a more stable, less personal and more efficient style of politics. Then, in 1978, Deng Xiaoping led China in the repudiation of Marxist economics and the development of a market-based economy. Only then, at last, was China ready for its own industrial revolution. Since 1978 China has moved several hundred million workers from jobs in which their work is worth $1 a day to jobs worth $20 a day. Like Britain 200 years ago and every industrialising country since, it has done this by taking people from subsistence farms and putting them in factories. From the economic historian's viewpoint there is nothing very special about what is happening in China; it is just doing what many others have done before. The only difference is the scale.

But scale makes all the difference. Never before has productivity increased in this way across a workforce this big. That means the economic arithmetic is starting to work in China's favour again: the nexus between population and economic size is being re-established, so that China will, if it keeps growing, once again become the biggest economy in the world.

*

The big question, then, is whether China will keep growing. On the economic fundamentals there is no reason why it shouldn't. China has become the second-richest country in the world by moving half of its workforce from the field to the factory. That means the other half – hundreds of millions of workers – are still back in the old semi-subsistence economy, ready and waiting to move to more productive jobs. If that happens, China can keep growing fast for another few decades. Of course, there will be bumps along the way: the Chinese economy is no more immune than any other to bubbles, crises, cycles and blunders. It seems to have ridden out the global financial crisis of the past few years to emerge in good shape, but there are plenty of traps ahead that may slow its growth. However, while these short and medium-term economic problems will be important to investors and exporters, they will not necessarily affect the long-term trends in China's economy that will shape Asia's strategic future. These are more likely to be threatened by problems beyond the economy itself.

We cannot be sure that China has really created a durable political and social basis for a high-productivity economy. Sceptics about China's future doubt it, and they may be right. No one has ever run a productivity revolution on this scale before, so no one knows for sure how to make it work. China faces social, political, demographic and environmental problems of unprecedented scale and complexity, and so there is a real chance that China will stumble. Equally, however, there is a real chance that it will not. It might be just as big a mistake to assume that China will not keep growing as to assume that it will, because, as real as China's problems are, none is a certain show-stopper.

China's biggest problems may turn out to be environmental, but they won't be China's alone. No one knows whether the planet can sustain 1.3 billion more people producing as much, and consuming as much, as we in the West now do. The problems seem even more daunting if you add a billion Indians and hundreds of millions more in other fast-growing economies. The challenge of curbing carbon emissions is the most obvious first hurdle to sustainable mass prosperity in the Asian century, but supplies of oil, gas and many other minerals will also become critical if consumption in China and other emerging economies keeps growing. This is not just China's problem: we will all feel the pressure as demand increases for all kinds of resources, just as the pressure to cut carbon emissions will press down on all of us. China will be no worse placed to compete for resources than other countries.

Likewise, China has serious demographic problems. Its population is ageing because of the one-child policy. Nonetheless, it still has the world's largest workforce by far, and if the shift of Chinese workers from low to high-productivity jobs can be maintained, a shortage of workers will not stop China reaching the top of the economic table in the next few decades. The demographics that favour China today will only start working against it later in the twenty-first century, when India's transformation gathers speed and its population overtakes that of China. But by then China will have been the world's most economically powerful country for half a century.

However, to get there China must manage immense social stresses. Hundreds of millions of lives are being transformed faster than we can easily imagine. People whose parents never used a telephone now surf the net each night. At the same time hundreds of millions of others are excluded by changes that haven't touched them yet. Disorientation among the first group, and resentment among the second, are no doubt stressing Chinese society, posing risks to stability and perhaps jeopardising future growth. The resentment of those who have so far been left behind may be manageable as long as they hope and expect that their turn will come. The aspirations of those already swept along in the whirlwind of change might be harder to manage, because they may offer a direct challenge to China's political system.

This is the great conundrum of China's rise. Many people in the West doubt that China's government can deliver sustained economic growth because it is communist. They may be right, but it is a more complex issue than this simple analysis suggests. There are two possibilities to consider. One is that China can defy history and keep growing under its present political system. The other is that it might change that system and keep growing anyway.

China's ruling party is much more Leninist than communist. It has abandoned all the old ideological baggage except Lenin's doctrine of one-party rule; but the Leninist legacy alone might mean that China's economic miracle cannot last. No country before has sustained economic growth for long with a political system based on such a narrow and jealously guarded monopoly of power. Many therefore predict that China cannot keep growing unless its politics become freer – and that the longer the party holds out, the more likely it becomes that China will stumble. However, you can turn this argument around. China is the first Leninist state to have successfully run a market economy, and therefore the first to enjoy the legitimacy conferred by sustained economic growth. There is no precedent for China's unique version of market-Leninism. We do not know whether it will survive, but we do know that it has survived so far. Since 1978 the Chinese Communist Party has successfully presided over an economic transformation of unparalleled size.

After thirty years the Chinese model can no longer be dismissed as a freakish and unsustainable anomaly. Nor is it inflexible: while its Leninist core has remained sacrosanct, the rest of the system has already changed a great deal over the past few decades. And it will need to keep changing, because it seems likely that people in China will want more say in politics as they get richer, if only because that is what has happened everywhere else as economies have grown.

The party appears to recognise that changes will be needed, but it finds it hard to say what the changes might be, how fast they will happen, and how far they will go. China's leaders will be very cautious. They want to maintain their own position, of course, but they also want to avoid the instability and indeed chaos that remain for them an ever-present risk in a country as large and complex and potentially unruly as theirs. China's leaders often seem paranoid about unrest, but we can hardly be surprised that they are risk-averse, given the turbulence of China's past and the bewildering challenges of the present. Governing 1.3 billion people through the biggest, fastest economic and social transformation in history must be an anxious business, and it would make anyone cautious.

Nonetheless, they also know that they cannot take their popular legit-imacy for granted, and that some gradual liberalisation of politics may be essential to keep the party in power and China growing. The real question, then, is not whether China reforms politically, but whether the party can strike a balance between keeping power and control on the one hand, and allowing enough reform to retain its legitimacy on the other. It will not be easy, because the leaders have a lot to juggle: preserving their position, satisfying popular aspirations for political participation, while keeping China peaceful and prosperous. Whether they succeed depends in part on the Chinese people themselves. Will they go on accepting that the party knows best, and let the Politburo set the pace of reform? Or will they demand faster change than their leaders are willing to allow?

It would be remarkable if China found a solution to this quintessential political conundrum other than by trial and error, which will involve at least some unrest. Indeed, we see this already today. Yet it is quite possible that a workable balance will be found between conservatism and reform. It is quite possible that China's leaders and people will negotiate political reforms that meet aspirations for popular participation, preserve order and keep the economy on track. Many other countries have managed exactly this kind of process.

It is the haunting image of Tiananmen Square twenty years ago that makes us doubt this will happen in China. Tiananmen enshrines an image of a party set in ruthless and implacable opposition to the welfare and aspirations of its people. If this image is true, there can be no basis for compromise on either side between party and people on the pace and direction of reform. But is this true in China today? People everywhere have complex and ambivalent attitudes to their governments, and certainly China is no exception. There is a lot of grumbling, and a lot to grumble about. But there is another side of the ledger, too. Hundreds of millions of people in China today lead better lives than they did twenty years ago thanks to their country's economic and social transformation. They have more and better food to eat, live in better houses, are more economically secure, with better health care, better education and more personal opportunities than they have ever known before. It is uncomfortable to say it, but in half a lifetime the Chinese Communist Party has presided over the biggest increase in human welfare in history. For half a billion people, they have indeed "made poverty history," and seem set to do the same for another half-billion in the future.

This presents us with a perplexing moral calculation. Many bad things are done by the Chinese government: minorities are repressed, dissent ruthlessly stifled. But the same government has done a great deal to improve the lives of the vast majority of Chinese people. How does the balance stand between good and bad? Outside China, the bad weighs heavily. We see the repression as unnecessary for China's growth, serving only to preserve the party's power. But we can hardly be surprised that within China the balance is viewed differently. Many Chinese people agree with their government that freer politics carries too high a risk of instability, and they naturally place a high value on the economic and social progress that stability has provided.

We might disagree with these judgments, but when we are assessing the durability of China's political system, it is their judgments, not ours, that count. The Chinese themselves have an immense stake in China's present success, so they have an immense stake in keeping it going. That means the pressure for political reform in China need not play out like the collapse of communism in Eastern Europe. The Chinese might well find a way to balance their desire for democracy and their desire to keep enjoying the benefits of stability and growth. If so, the Chinese people and their leaders will be able to negotiate the pace and direction of political change to keep China growing. Those who expect that a thirst for democracy will somehow stop China's rise, and therefore prevent China challenging America's primacy in Asia, may be disappointed. We cannot be sure that China will keep growing, but we need to recognise that it quite possibly will.

CHINA'S CHOICES

In the long run, economics is what counts in power politics. National power has many manifestations – military, political, cultural – but only one ultimate source. No country in history has exercised great power without great wealth, and the country with the most wealth always ends up with the most power. The wealth that matters is the aggregate wealth of the state, rather than that of individuals. That is why, while China's per-capita income will lag far behind the West's for decades if not longer, China's political and strategic weight in the world will depend on its overall, rather than per-capita, GDP.

This does not mean that if China overtakes the US to become the biggest economy in the world, it will automatically take over America's role as the unipolar global power. China will not rule the world, no matter how much it grows, because there are too many other strong states to contend with. America, Japan, India, Europe and perhaps Russia will all be powerful enough to seriously limit China's global influence, as might some of the emerging powers. For some decades to come China's rise will have by far its biggest impact in Asia, and that, obviously, is where the implications for Australia will play out too.

In Asia, China's growing power undermines the stable US-led order because the stronger it becomes, the more influence it will seek to wield and the less it will accept American leadership. But, you might ask, why would China want to do that? China's leaders are focused internally. Their priority is to maintain political stability and that requires economic growth. Asia's order has served them well by fostering growth up until now, and they have no reason to upset it. All this is true, but only up to a point. China's leaders do want peace and order so they can keep growing, but they face other pressures too. Their people want China to be strong, respected and influential as well as rich. The leaders want these things for China too.

They are no different in this from people and leaders in other countries.

We all want our country to have influence and respect commensurate with our strength, although in the Chinese case these emotions may be amplified by pride in their glorious past and present achievements, and by the memory of relatively recent humiliations. It therefore seems very unlikely that, as China's economy grows to match America's, its people will still willingly accept a subordinate position to America. They expect their leaders to make China strong as well as wealthy, and if necessary, like the citizens of almost any other country, they will be willing to sacrifice material interests for the sake of international status. The richer they become, the more impatient they will be for their leaders to assert a bigger role for China in Asia.

The surprise is that China has not staked a bigger claim for influence already. This, in part, is tactics. Time is on China's side, because the longer it waits, the more power it will have and the stronger its bargaining position becomes. Even today, China remains careful not to confront American power too overtly, hoping to delay the showdown until its challenge is irresistible. That time may be fast approaching, and meanwhile the benefits to China of American primacy are dwindling. China now has much less to fear from Russia, Japan and even America than it did in 1972, and China no longer depends on American favour for access to the global economy.

Already China needs US leadership in Asia much less than before, but what does it want instead? The answer is not as simple as you might think. Of course China wants as much influence as it can get, but it also wants to live in peace. There is an inherent tension between these two aims: the more China grasps for influence, the greater the risk of instability. Beijing must therefore strike a balance, looking for a new role in Asia that maximises its influence while minimising disorder. Some people, especially in America, say that what China wants is impossible. They believe that US primacy is the only possible basis for stability in Asia, and that any attempt by China to seek more influence at America's expense will plunge the region into chaos. That may have been true in the past, but China's leaders do not accept that it will be true in future. They believe a new order could be built that keeps Asia peaceful and yet gives China more influence.

*

The Chinese do not talk much about how they see this new Asian order and their place in it. Probably they do not have a clear idea themselves, and are making it up as they go. However, we can know something about their aspirations and their circumstances, and these give us a rough idea of their options and the choices they might make in the next few decades.

The least likely possibility is that China will try to impose on Asia a harsh hegemony backed by armed force and political repression. It is easy to assume that the Politburo would naturally incline to a repressive foreign policy simply because they are communists, but the evidence is against it. China's diplomacy can be strident and assertive, and occasionally it is backed with armed force in places like the South China Sea, but it shows no sign of hoping to build a Stalinist empire. Taiwan, of course, is the exception, but it is a special case because the Chinese see it as part of China, and we accept that claim. That means it is probably too pessimistic to take Taiwan as a pointer to China's future international conduct. Still, we shouldn't be complacent. No doubt some Chinese would like their country to establish a firm leadership in Asia and would be happy enough to use force to do so. Even if the present Chinese government seems to have more modest aspirations, there is always a risk that future leaders will become more ambitious as their power grows. The best guarantee that they will not go this way is that they will not have enough power to do so. Even at its most powerful, China will face other states in Asia – Japan, India and probably the US – strong enough to make it very expensive, if not impossible, for it to rule the region on its own terms. Beijing would find that the more harshly it tried to dominate Asia, the more opposition it would face from these powers. It is therefore much more likely that China will see its interests better served by aiming lower.

In recent years the Chinese have looked closely at the histories of previous rising powers for ideas about what they should do. One case they have probably studied carefully is recent history's best example of cost-effective hegemony: America in the western hemisphere. Since 1824, under what is called the Monroe Doctrine, America has exercised uncontested primacy over the entire western hemisphere, managing affairs from Alaska to Tierra del Fuego to suit its own interests without fighting major wars or occupying major countries. This is not an old-style empire. America's neighbours are more or less free to run their own countries in their own way, but Washington insists its views are given full consideration on any issues that touch American interests, and American interests always take precedence over anyone's from outside the hemisphere. If the Central Committee in Beijing could engineer something like this in Asia, they would get plenty of influence with a minimum of disorder and relatively little cost. It would be diplomatically neat too: America could hardly complain that China was violating any fundamental tenets of international morality if it were simply following America's example. And such an approach would resonate with China's own history: the traditional tributary relations between imperial China and its Asian neighbours bear some resemblance to America's soft Monroe Doctrine hegemony.

It would be much easier for Beijing to establish this kind of soft hegemony in Asia than to build a repressive empire because it would meet much less opposition. China's smaller and middle-size neighbours might not like the idea of living in China's orbit, but they could come to accept it as better than the alternatives. Australia might take that view too. It is even possible that America could eventually decide to leave Asia to be run by a relatively benevolent China, especially if it remained open to American trade and investment. India might likewise decide to leave East Asia to China, choosing instead to establish its own sphere of influence in West Asia and the Middle East. Japan, however, remains the big stumbling block, because it has nowhere else to go. Japan would find it very hard to accept China as the leading power in Asia, and itself as one of China's followers. For all its problems, Japan is still a formidable power. The Japanese are too proud, too distrustful of China and too aware of their own strength to accept Chinese leadership willingly. Even after two decades of stagnation and facing deep demographic problems, Japan remains a very rich, technologically advanced country with great strategic potential – including the capacity to build nuclear weapons. The Chinese cannot simply ignore Japan. Nor can they contain it by force or placate it by charm. In the end Japanese resistance would make it impossible for China to become Asia's soft hegemon; it would find itself sliding instead into a costly power struggle. They need to look for a third model.

If China cannot exercise sole leadership in Asia without meeting great resistance, its best approach may be to share power in a collective leadership with Asia's other strong states. This could maximise its influence at minimum cost and risk. Collective leadership by a group of great powers is an unusual but not unprecedented model of regional order. The most famous and successful example was the Concert of Europe, which emerged after the Napoleonic wars to avoid the dangers of the old balance-of-power system that had kept Europe at war for much of the eighteenth century. It worked for almost a hundred years and provided the foundation for Europe's spectacular rise to dominate the globe in the nineteenth century. The concert model is based on the simple idea that when a number of strong states compete for power and influence, they are all better off if they agree that none will try to dominate, and instead all share power more or less equally.

An agreement like this is called a "concert of power." It can last only as long as all parties understand that if any one of them tries to take control, the others will fight to prevent this, and that the resulting war will cost more than any possible gains are worth. Even so, such agreements are inherently precarious. To keep the concert intact, the parties must be very careful in their relations with one another. They must accept the legitimacy of one another's political systems, even when they are very different. They must stay out of one another's internal affairs. They must accept the validity of one another's international interests, and be prepared to compromise to reach a deal where these interests collide. They must accept that each member will have armed forces that can limit the strategic options of the others. In other words, they must all sit at the table as equals in status, even if not in power. And for this arrangement to be credible and enduring, only the strongest powers in a system can have a seat at the table.

If China realises that it could only dominate Asia at the cost of intense rivalry and possibly major war, it might settle instead for a place at a table like this. But it would not be happy about it. A "Concert of Asia" would offer the Chinese people much less than they would like, and much less than many would probably expect. There would therefore be bitter opposition to settling for so little. We can imagine the arguments: when China becomes the strongest power in the world, why shouldn't it be acknowledged as the undisputed leader of Asia? Why should it have to sit down with the Americans, the Indians and especially the Japanese and treat them as equals? If Beijing is willing to overlook these arguments and settle for a seat in a concert, it will only be because it recognises a good deal when it sees one. This option would give China a lot more influence than it has today, and it would cost a lot less than a bid for primacy. If China's leaders are thinking rationally about their options, this argument might prevail. But it would be China's absolute minimum. As its power approaches America's, we can be sure that Beijing will not settle for less than a place among equals in a collective leadership for Asia. It would rather risk greater disorder than accept that it has no more influence than it was accorded in 1972. The question, then, is whether the other great powers are prepared to concede that much. In particular, will America be prepared to sit down with China as an equal?

Asia's security and Australia's future depend not just on the choices China might make, but on America's choices too. Even if China overtakes it economically over the next few decades, the US will remain the second-strongest country in the world for a long time to come, and by far the most serious constraint on Chinese power. The way America chooses to use its power is as important as anything China decides, and America's choices may be harder than China's. A peaceful new order in Asia to accommodate China's growing power can only be built if America is willing to allow China some political and strategic space. Such concessions do not often happen. History offers few examples of a rising power finding its place in the international order without a war with the dominant power. Conflict is only avoided when the dominant power willingly makes space for the challenger, as Britain made way for America in the late nineteenth century. Will America do the same for China? Should it?

As America confronts these questions, it too faces a choice between influence and order. Like China, it wants as much influence as it can get, with as little disorder as possible, so it has to balance its desire for Asia to remain peaceful against its desire to remain in charge. Washington has not faced this choice before. Since Nixon went to China, US primacy has been synonymous with order, and the more influence America has had, the more stable Asia has been. Now China's rise means that the region might be more peaceful if America settles for a more modest role. If instead America tries to retain primacy in the face of China's power, it will provoke a struggle that upsets the region. It would be sacrificing Asia's peace to preserve its own primacy.

America could easily find itself doing just that. After being in charge for forty years, many Americans cannot imagine that Asia can be peaceful except under American leadership. Conceding even a share of power to another country looks risky, and especially conceding power to China. It is easy to see any desire by China to expand its influence as inherently threatening, and the more repressive and authoritarian China's government appears, the more threatening it looks. No one can be comfortable about a regime that represses dissent at home exercising more power abroad. But what is the alternative? Forty years ago Washington – and Canberra – decided to accept the Chinese Communist Party as the legitimate government of China. Since then, and partly as a result, China has grown to become a very powerful country indeed. As America continues to deal with China and to benefit from its growth, it faces the consequences of those decisions. Some of those are unpalatable. While continuing to accept the communists as the legitimate government of China internally, many Americans would now prefer to deny that China's government can legitimately exercise its power internationally.

Unfortunately, Americans do not get to make that kind of choice now. They cannot separate China's internal government from the exercise of its international power. China's power, controlled by China's government, must be dealt with as a simple fact of international politics. If Americans deny China the right to exercise its power internationally within the same limits and norms that they accept for themselves, they can hardly be surprised if China decides not to accept the legitimacy of American power and starts pushing back. These days it can push back pretty hard.

America, therefore, has to decide whether its reasons for trying to prevent China exercising its growing power on the international stage are strong enough to justify the resulting mayhem. That depends on whether China is willing to exercise its power within the rules accepted by the international community as a whole – broadly those set out in the Charter of the United Nations. So far the evidence suggests that it will. The fact that China's government is repressive at home makes us uneasy, but it does not automatically mean it will behave unacceptably abroad. The mere fact that China wants to expand its influence as its power grows does not show that it intends to break the rules and use that power improperly. In particular, the fact that China's ambitions might be contrary to American interests does not make them inherently illegitimate –

unless you believe, as many Americans do, that acceptable international conduct is defined as the acceptance of American primacy.

Americans find that easy to believe because they have got so used to exercising primacy and they don't want to give it up. It has become a matter of national identity, which makes it very hard to relinquish. What's more, they do not yet accept that they will have to fight to keep it. Most Americans, even those who know Asia well, do not really accept that China poses a serious challenge to their power and role in Asia. They remind you that America's eclipse in Asia has been predicted many times before, and the doomsayers have always been wrong. They say this time will be no different: America will bounce back from its present troubles, stronger than ever.

This is half right. It is true that America's present problems will pass. The wars in Iraq and Afghanistan have been wasteful and demoralising, but they will not bring America to its knees. America's economic problems are serious and debilitating, but it remains a remarkably innovative and vibrant place with an immense capacity for recovery and reinvention. If China's challenge to America depended on American weakness, there would be little to worry about. But the story of Asia's power shift is not about America. It is about China. This is not a story of American weakness, but of Chinese strength. Even if the War on Terror and the global financial crisis had never happened, even if America's budget was in healthy surplus and its financial system in perfect shape, China's economic transformation would still pose the biggest threat to America's place at the apex of global power since it reached there in 1880.

China's challenge is different because never before has there been a country with the potential to overtake America economically. Japan could not do it: with only one-third America's population, Japan's workers would have needed to be three times as productive as America's to overtake it, and that was never going to happen. The Soviet Union's bigger population gave it a better chance, but its economy never approached America's level of productivity. China is different because its population is much bigger than America's and its economy works much better than the Soviet Union's.

Even so, all of us find it hard to imagine that America's economy could ever be overtaken. It seems a contradiction in terms: an America that was not the world's richest and most powerful nation would not be America. This is not true – America as number two would still be America – but it will take most Americans some time to accept this, and the process will be a painful one.

*

One way to cope with the prospect of relative economic decline is to focus on other forms of power. America will have by far the world's strongest military for a long time to come. Perhaps the huge gap between US and Chinese military power will make up for the narrowing gap in economic power – but the closer you look, the less credible that becomes. With armed force, what matters is not what you've got, but what you can do with it. America still has the biggest defence budget, the most aircraft carriers and the stealthiest fighters in the world. These forces give it a global military reach that China will not be able to match for many decades, if ever. But when we look at what America can actually do with its military in Asia, it is clear that the balance is shifting China's way quite fast. For decades America has exercised what the naval strategists call "sea control" in the Western Pacific. This means simply that the US can defend its ships from other navies and air forces well enough to be able to send forces by sea around the Pacific to wherever they are needed, without any Asian power being able to stop them. This has never given the US unlimited strategic power in Asia, because it always found land wars in Asia hard, as Korea and Vietnam showed. But Asia is a maritime theatre, and America's control of the sea has allowed it to exercise decisive strategic influence relatively cheaply.

Since the mid-1990s, however, this has started to change. China has invested heavily in naval and air forces, and with technology bought from

Russia it has developed substantial new capabilities. It is still no match for the US in overall maritime power, but China can now challenge American sea control where it matters most – in the waters close to China. It has been easier than you might expect because a contest for sea control is a very asymmetrical business. A country trying to achieve sea control must defend its ships against many different threats, wherever and whenever they might appear. The country trying to impede sea control – what the strategists call "sea denial" – has a much easier task; it can choose the method, time and place of attack that suits it best. And often it doesn't need to attack at all: the possibility that ships might be sunk can raise the cost and risk of naval operations high enough to make them impracticable.

China is developing very cost-effective sea-denial capabilities. The most important so far is a growing fleet of modern, quiet, lethal submarines. The most exotic and intriguing is an experimental system to attack large ships such as aircraft carriers with ballistic missiles. If that works, it could be a game-changer. Already China has raised the cost and risk of US naval operations in the seas around China. Robert Gates, the US secretary of defence, recently acknowledged that America can no longer assume that it has sea control in the Western Pacific. The longer-term trends are running China's way, too. It will be much cheaper for China to expand its capacity to sink US ships than for the US to improve its capacity to defend them, and in any case America's fiscal deficits severely limit how much more it can spend over the next decade.

This does not mean that China is anywhere near being able to replace America as the dominant maritime power in Asia. China is acquiring an effective sea-denial capability, but it has no chance of being able to achieve sea control for itself. The asymmetries that make it relatively easy for China to threaten US ships also make it very easy for the US to threaten China's, and that will remain true for as far ahead as we can see. In fact, quite a few other countries in Asia – Japan, India, South Korea, Singapore and Australia – have substantial and growing sea-denial capabilities. That means the Western Pacific is likely to become a kind of naval no-go zone in coming decades; many countries will be capable of sea-denial, but not even the US will be able to achieve sea control. That limits China's capacity to project power around the region in support of any bid for primacy, but it also erodes the military foundations of America's primacy, just as its economic foundations are being eroded by China's economic growth.

There is a deeper point here. Even if America makes a massive effort to reverse the trends and rebuild a sea-control capability in the Western Pacific, would that make much difference to its long-term position in Asia? Would it make sense for America to try to sustain primacy in Asia by force of arms? Can it impose by force a primacy which it no longer has the economic power to command? What kind of primacy would that be? What kind of country would that make America?

*

Today, of course, America still has more than money and military force on its side. Despite periodic outbreaks of anti-Americanism, it has a lot of soft power, and the admiration and trust of other countries is an important asset. American diplomacy in Asia over the past decade has banked on this, assuming that the stronger China grows, the more nervous other countries in Asia will become and the more eagerly they will welcome American leadership and protection. Building on the network of alliances it established in the Cold War, America hopes that the support of China's neighbours will help to redress the shift in economic and strategic weight. This makes good sense as far as it goes. Many Asian countries are wary of China and would like America to stay engaged to balance Beijing and prevent it dominating the region – but that does not mean they will automatically support American primacy on America's terms.

While most of America's potential supporters are democracies, and hence seem natural allies, they also have important relationships with China. Like Australia, they do not want to choose. They will support

America so long as that does not damage links with China, but the support will quickly soften if choices between Washington and Beijing have to be made. That means the more uncompromising America becomes towards China, the less support it can expect to receive from other Asian nations. Asians care much more about peace and stability than they do about American primacy *per se*. They would far prefer America to make room for China and keep Asia peaceful than to confront China and risk conflict just to protect its status. That means they will support America to *balance* China, but not to *dominate* it.

India is the key here, because in the long run it is America's most powerful potential ally against China, and it is already one of only two countries – alongside Japan – big enough to count much in the regional power balance against China. Americans hope that India's fear of China and its commitment to democracy will see it automatically line up behind America. But that seems unlikely: India is a great power with its own agenda, ambitious to build its influence rather than simply support American leadership. It will want to manage its critical relationship with Beijing to suit its interests, not support America's.

Japan is different. It probably will support America against China, and it remains a huge strategic asset, but the price may be high because Japan faces a very difficult situation. Like everyone in Asia, Japan has come to depend on China to bolster its economy, but Japan fears China's rise more than others. The two countries have deep animosities which seem hard to transcend, and Japan fears that as China grows stronger, it will squeeze Japan, politically, economically and strategically. Although Japan has the economic weight and technological depth to be a major power in Asia, for the past sixty-five years it has instead accepted a dependent position as America's strategic client. That has worked for the Japanese because they have been sure that America would always put Japan's interests ahead of China's.

China's rise and Japan's relative decline undermine that. As China becomes more important, Japan becomes less confident that America will always put it first. And the Japanese fear that the closer America and China become, the less America will help them resist Chinese pressure. As a result, Japan finds itself in a paradoxical predicament: the worse America and China get on, the more secure it feels. A good, stable, trusting relationship between Beijing and Washington would be threatening to Tokyo, so – perhaps alone among America's friends and allies in Asia – Japan is likely to push America towards confrontation with China, rather than towards accommodation. The only alternative for Japan would be to stop relying on America for security and emerge as a major power in its own right. That would not be easy, but it is far from unthinkable. Meanwhile, for as long as it lasts, Japan's support is a liability as well as an asset for America, because it will nudge America towards confrontation with China.

*

Back in the mid-1990s, when people first wondered whether China might one day challenge American power, there seemed an easy answer. China needed access to the global economy for finance, technology, markets and raw materials, and America directly or indirectly controlled this access. So if China started to challenge America – economically, militarily or politically – its rise could be stopped simply by shutting it out of the global system. This made sense as long as China's economy didn't matter too much to America. But it made less and less sense as China grew and America became more and more dependent on it to keep its own economy afloat. Today, of course, China has become too important to everyone's economies, including America's, for the weapon ever to be used.

   This cuts both ways, because China depends more and more on the US economy too. There is an economic "balance of terror" between them: neither side can do anything that damages the other's economy without doing at least as much harm to its own. Strategically, however, this interdependence is a bigger problem for Washington because it has lost the lever with which it hoped to prevent the challenge to its power. Now it cannot escape the dilemma that a strong and growing China is both vital to America's economy and a threat to its international leadership.

A great deal has been written in America about China's rise, and in the last few years more and more writers have acknowledged that a historic power shift is underway. But the debate about how to respond has not moved forward much since these ideas from the mid-1990s. Americans have always been divided between optimists and pessimists about China. The pessimists believe that if China keeps growing, then − like every rising power throughout history − it will challenge the *status quo*, leading inevitably to conflict with America. The optimists expect that China's growing power will be peacefully accommodated in the existing regional order, leaving US leadership intact, because that is in everybody's best interests. Both optimists and pessimists agree, however, that America should respond to China with a policy they call "hedging." The essence of hedging is that America will accept and accommodate China's growing power so long as China does not challenge US primacy; otherwise America must and will do whatever it takes to defend and maintain its position.

The hedging policy has lasted for fifteen years now, for several reasons. First, it appeals to both pessimists and optimists alike. Although they differ over which option China will choose − the optimists think it will continue to accept US leadership, the pessimists think it will challenge it − both camps agree that China's rise should be tolerated only so long as Beijing respects US primacy. Second, hedging means America does not have to do anything, because it shifts the onus onto China to choose whether it accepts or challenges US primacy. Third, it assumes that whatever China chooses, America still ends up on top. You can see why Americans like it.

It is also easy to express. US governments present the hedging policy in two-word slogans. The Bush administration's slogan was "Responsible Stakeholder" and Obama's seems to be "Strategic Reassurance." Both reflect the bipartisan assumption in US political and policy circles that US primacy is non-negotiable. It is hard to know whether this approach has been seriously re-examined over the past fifteen years as China has kept growing, but the evidence suggests not. The day-to-day management of the relationship gets a lot of detailed attention, but presidents and other senior figures avoid substantial analysis of America's long-term intentions towards China. One reason is 9/11. For almost a decade, America's political leaders have convinced themselves that a small group of fugitives on the run in Pakistan poses a bigger challenge to America's place in the world than the economic transformation of the world's most populous country. Future historians will find that hard to explain.

Only in 2009 did this start to change. The global financial crisis made the wider implications of China's success impossible to ignore. It confronted Washington with the sheer scale and dynamism of the Chinese economy and the increasing clout it gave China in international decision-making. It showed that treating China just as one more "responsible stakeholder" in the international system was no longer possible. When Obama visited China in November 2009, it seems he hoped his personal magnetism would warm China to his view of Asia's future under US leadership. Instead he came away with a new and clearer sense that Chinese power was not going to fit comfortably into America's world. Just two weeks after his return from China, Obama, announcing the long-awaited troop surge, set a deadline to start pulling US forces out of Afghanistan. He explained the need for a deadline carefully in his speech. He said that although the struggle against terrorism was important, it was not the only or the greatest struggle America faced. America had

> failed to appreciate the connection between our national security and our economy … competition within the global economy has grown more fierce … We must rebuild our strength here at home. Our prosperity provides a foundation for our power. It pays for our military. It underwrites our diplomacy … it will allow us to compete

in this century as successfully as we did in the last. That is why our troop commitment in Afghanistan cannot be open-ended – because the nation that I am most interested in building is our own.

Here for the first time since 9/11 an American president started to explain to his people that the shifting weight of the global economy would shape America's place in the world more than the threat of terrorism. He did not mention China, but in December 2009 he did not have to. Two weeks later, in Copenhagen, the message was hammered home as China flexed its muscles again. The comfortable assumption that one way or another China can be persuaded or compelled to accept American leadership – in Asia or more broadly – no longer seems so credible in Washington. Inside the Beltway it is time to rethink the hedging strategy and ask what America should do if China refuses to accept its leadership.

AMERICA'S CHOICES

America has three options for responding to China's rise. It can withdraw from Asia, share power with China, or compete with it for primacy. The least likely choice for America is to make way for China by withdrawing, at least if you believe what American leaders say. Ever since the end of the Cold War, they have been resolutely affirming their determination to stay. They say America has more reason than ever to be engaged in the world's most dynamic region, especially as it is so important to them economically. Nonetheless, withdrawal is possible, not in the form of a sudden and complete retreat to Hawaii, but gradually. Over the next few decades, as the changing balance between the costs and benefits of American engagement becomes clearer, successive administrations might take decisions which cumulatively amount to the same thing. That would never happen while America's place in Asia is uncontested, because without competitors the costs of leadership are low and the benefits are high. However, the calculation changes as the situation changes. Sharing power with China or competing with it will be much less appealing to America than the primacy of recent decades. The more China's power grows, and the more it costs the US to maintain primacy, the more seriously Americans will ask whether they still need to play a big role in Asia.

One reason they might is economics. Asia will remain important to America's prosperity, and stability is vital to Asia's growth, so Americans have long argued that their own prosperity requires them to stay engaged to keep the peace. However, that purpose defeats itself if staying engaged in Asia leads to a destabilising contest with China. It only makes economic sense for America to stay engaged if it can find a way to avoid competing with China. We will see soon what that might be.

A stronger reason for America to stay engaged in Asia might be to protect the United States itself. Ultimately, Americans believe their security depends on preventing any country in Europe or Asia from becoming powerful enough to threaten the American homeland by projecting its power over the Pacific or Atlantic oceans. They fought the great wars of the last century in Europe and Asia to stop that happening. Does America have to remain engaged in Asia to prevent a similar massive threat emerging in future? It is not clear that it does. The Nazis and Soviets threatened to dominate the whole Eurasian landmass, but no Asian power, including China, poses that kind of risk. As we have seen, China has little chance of dominating Asia, let alone the whole of Eurasia, because it faces formidable competition from Japan, India and probably Russia. America could leave all these countries to maintain a balance of power among themselves, intervening only to restore the balance if it looked like being overwhelmed by a single hegemon. The British used this approach – strategists call it "offshore balancing" – very successfully for centuries in Europe, and America could do the same.

This would not be good news for Asia, of course. Asia's major powers are much more likely to build stable and peaceful relationships if the US is present to lend its weight to a shared regional leadership. It is true that if America stays and competes with China, Asia will be less stable. But if America could be persuaded to stay engaged without competing with China, that would offer a much better chance for stability. This is America's second option.

Like China, America will find it hard to get all it wants in Asia over the next few decades. America would like to keep regional leadership, but China has the capacity to make that very costly. Like China, therefore, it might consider sharing power as the best way to balance the ambition for influence with the need for order. We saw before how a Concert of Asia might work. It is probably the best strategic future available for Asia over the next few decades, but it will also be the hardest to bring about, and convincing America to accept it will be the hardest part of all.

To share power with China, America will have to deal with China as an equal. The more you think about that, the harder it seems. America would have to abandon its residual doubts about the legitimacy of China's political system and become much more circumspect about criticising its internal affairs. That means no more lecturing China about dissidents, Tibet or religious freedom. It would have to accept that China's international interests will legitimately differ from America's, and be prepared to compromise to settle those differences amicably. That means no more lecturing China about its failure to meet US expectations on matters such as Iran, Sudan and North Korea. And America would have to accept that China has a right to build armed forces as large and capable as America's in order to defend its interests. That means no more lecturing China about excessive defence spending or lack of transparency about its military plans. In short, it means surrendering primacy and all that goes with it.

For most Americans, treating China as a trustworthy equal is simply unthinkable. Partly that says something about the way they see China. To many Americans, and many others, China is untrustworthy simply because it is communist. But China is not North Korea – for many years China has been a reliable if not always congenial international actor. We may not like all the polices it has pursued, but it has consistently done what it said it would do. Of course, that is no guarantee that China will always be trustworthy, but we have at least a starting point to build the kind of relationship that would make a shared leadership in Asia workable. And what is the alternative? Are we saying we simply cannot work with people whose political systems and values are different from ours? Trust always carries risks, but not trusting carries risks too, and costs. Those who say we cannot work with China need to be sure they understand what the alternatives to trust are, and the costs and risks that would follow. If the alternative is confrontation, that is a high price to pay.

To some this will sound like appeasement. For seventy years "appeasement" has been the most powerful three syllables in international affairs, able to stop a policy debate dead. It stands for a simple precept: accommodating any country trying to expand its influence and power is always wrong. The lesson of Munich is that making concessions to ambitious powers only encourages more demands, which, if met, will eventually destroy the international order. Firm refusal, on the other hand, compels respect for the existing order and keeps the peace. It is easy to see how this might apply to China today. If we concede a greater share of regional leadership to China, it will only want more in future. Eventually Beijing will make demands the rest of us cannot accept, and we will have to go to war to stop it. Better to draw the line now by refusing to concede any further regional influence to China than it already has, even if that leads to conflict. Better a smaller war now than a bigger one later.

But this might be to misinterpret the lesson of Munich. Perhaps Chamberlain's mistake was not that he accommodated Hitler over Czechoslovakia. He was, after all, right to fear war with Germany and to want to avoid it if possible. His mistake was that he did not prevent the even bigger war that broke out twelve months later, by failing to make it absolutely clear that there would be no accommodation over Poland. Had he done that, World War II could quite possibly have been avoided. This has important implications for the approach to China. As we saw earlier, China's ambitions will depend on how Beijing calculates the balance between the costs and the benefits of different options. The rest of us in Asia, including America, can influence its calculations by what we do. The more space we allow China, the less it gains by reaching for more than we are willing to give. The more we can convince Beijing of the high cost of reaching beyond that limit, the less likely it is to conclude that the gains of a more aggressive policy would be worth it. This suggests the best way to manage China's ambitions is both to offer it enough to be reasonably satisfied and to make absolutely clear that further demands will meet determined resistance from a regional coalition, one prepared to use force if necessary to prevent any Chinese attempt to use its power aggressively.

A Concert of Asia would be a very effective way to manage China's rise in this way, because it provides a framework to set and enforce the limits of acceptable international behaviour. In fact, a concert system cannot work without such limits being set and upheld, if necessary by force. That is what keeps the concert together. One of the hardest parts of negotiating a concert is to agree on what the limits should be, but that is easier today than it was in the past. The US and China – and India and Japan – have all subscribed to a broad set of rules for international conduct. It is called the Charter of the United Nations. The charter is a strange document which has gone a bit out of fashion, but it provides just the kind of rules we need as the basis for a concert of power. That makes the issue of trust easier to manage, because at least all parties start by agreeing on the rules they promise to abide by.

It is possible that America might learn to trust China in this kind of setting, if only because China's conduct would be constrained by the strength of others as well as by its own goodwill. But that is only part of the problem in establishing a concert system in Asia, because American doubts about treating China as an equal stem not only from how they see China, but also from how they see themselves. Exceptionalism is funda-mental to Americans' image of their country. The rest of us may smile condescendingly, but we cannot understand US foreign policy without recognising that Americans simply do not accept that theirs is just one country among others. They see it as exceptional, both materially and morally. From this flows an idea which is as old as America itself: the compromises and deal-making of old-style power politics are simply not the American way.

This is the deepest source of American resistance to sharing power with China. They believe that primacy is the only form of strategic engagement true to America's exceptional nature. They find it hard to imagine an America which is not the world's richest and most powerful state and the arbiter of global order. And they find it hard to conceive of America having to submit its interests and aspirations and ideals to the grubby compromises of power-political diplomacy. They believe that America has never operated this way before on the world stage, and they are proud of it. They will take a lot of persuading that America should change now.

In fact, this self-image is not strictly accurate. In 1945, at the apogee of American strength, the United States negotiated a new world order which had at its heart a concert of power. The five permanent members of the

United Nations Security Council, as originally conceived, constituted a concert of the great powers of the time. It did not end up working out that way, because the Cold War soon ruptured the deal and shifting power relativities rendered some of the members irrelevant. Nonetheless, the idea that America could work, as an equal, with other great powers to manage the international system was established in San Francisco. It was clear again in 1972 when Nixon went to China for a classic piece of old-style power politics. So America is capable of the pragmatism and the boldness that would be needed to share power in Asia with China. Nonetheless, it would be hard.

I often speak to Americans about this, and I put this catechism to them: "Do you think America should treat China as an equal if its power grows to equal America's?"

The answer is always "No."

Then I ask, "Do you think China will settle for anything less than being treated as an equal?"

The answer to that is always "No" too.

Then I ask, "So how do you expect the US and China to get along?"

I usually get a shrug by way of reply.

Those shrugs express America's third option: escalating competition with China. As China grows, America faces a choice of Euclidian clarity. If it will not withdraw from Asia, and if it will not share power with China, America must contest China's challenge to its leadership. That choice carries great costs – much greater, I think, than most Americans yet realise. Those costs would be justified if China tried to misuse its power to subjugate Asia. There is a risk, however, that America will slide into conflict with China, not to prevent Chinese hegemony but to pre-serve its own. Would it be worth making an adversary of China to avoid surrendering primacy and joining a Concert of Asia? If questions like this are soberly examined, the answer is almost certainly no, but sober examination is hard to arrange when one country challenges another. Emotions become engaged, and antagonism becomes the default setting.

The optimists push back against this gloom, arguing that Washington and Beijing both understand that their relationship is too important to both of them to allow strategic issues to upset it. As we have noted, economic interdependence does provide a huge incentive to keep the relationship positive and stable. But powerful forces push the other way, and America's hard choice between withdrawing from Asia, sharing power or competing with China must still be faced. The economic incentives will shape this choice, but not make it any easier. Economics will push both sides towards a power-sharing deal of some sort, but they will both still have to make big political sacrifices to get there. It is far from clear that they will make those sacrifices, especially if – in America's case, particularly – they do not yet clearly realise why they are worth making. The US risks drifting into strategic rivalry against China without weighing the costs.

What are those costs? What would rivalry between the US and China mean? We cannot be sure precisely, but some things are clear. China is already too powerful to be contained without intense and protracted pressure from America. That means committing more forces to Asia, an intensifying nuclear confrontation and building a bigger, more intense anti-China alliance in the region. Even if America does all this, China is unlikely simply to succumb. It would mount a determined and sustained resistance. The resulting antagonism could soon develop its own momentum, as each country reacted to the other. Military capabilities on both sides would grow quickly. Competition for influence and military bases in third countries would intensify, and it would be harder and harder for other countries to avoid taking sides. Asia would again face the prospect of a deep division between camps aligned with one or other of the two strongest powers. The conflict between these camps would inhibit trade, investment and travel, with immense economic costs. And there would be a real and growing risk of major war – even nuclear war – between them.

All of this sounds rather gloomy and surprising, because we do not have recent experience of serious strategic competition between really strong states. We have to go back to the last century for examples of how it might develop – the Cold War confrontation between the US and the Soviet Union, the European maelstroms of the first half of the twentieth century, or Asia's wars up until the 1970s. It would be wrong to assume that any increase in tension must lead to this kind of disaster, but it would be equally wrong to assume that Asia could never get that bad again. Any conflict between the US and China has a real chance of going nuclear. Nuclear war between the US and China would not be as bad as the holocaust we feared in the Cold War, but it could still quickly become the most deadly war in history. The stakes in Asia are very high indeed.

The American view of these stakes is coloured inevitably by victory in the Cold War. They tend to see this new contest as a re-run of their struggle against the Soviets, and assume they will win this one too. Many think China will be easier to beat because it behaves less threateningly and is less well-armed. That would be a mistake. China is fundamentally a more formidable long-term opponent than the Soviet Union because it is much richer. Many Americans do not see that, which makes them underestimate China, and makes them more eager to take it on as an adversary than they should be. Some may even welcome the idea. Everyone finds competition exhilarating, and many believe it brings out the best in us. Maybe that is true between people, but not between countries. In the 1940s, some Americans even welcomed the contest with the Soviet Union, before they realised just how dangerous it would become. George Kennan was the diplomat who conceived America's strategy of "containment." He was a good man who soon came to deplore the horror of the Cold War. But in 1947 he concluded his most famous essay with these chilling words:

> The issue of Soviet–American relations is in essence a test of the overall worth of the United States as a nation among nations. To avoid destruction the United States need only measure up to its own best traditions and prove itself worthy of preservation as a great nation.

Surely, there was never a fairer test of national quality than this. In the light of these circumstances, the thoughtful observer of Russian–American relations will find no cause for complaint in the Kremlin's challenge to American society. He will rather experience a certain gratitude to a Providence which, by providing the American people with this implacable challenge, has made their entire security as a nation dependent on their pulling themselves together and accepting the responsibilities of moral and political leadership that history plainly intended them to bear.

That was before the Soviets got nuclear weapons: Kennan's tone changed when the Kremlin could annihilate the United States. But this kind of thinking could touch a chord again today among those Americans who underestimate China as an adversary. That is easy to do. China doesn't need the immense military power of the Soviet Union to be very dangerous to America. If deterrence failed in a crisis – and deterrence is more fragile between China and the US than it was with the Soviets – a nuclear attack even with China's small arsenal could devastate major cities on the US West Coast: Los Angeles, San Francisco, Seattle. Americans should not slide into competition with China without assessing these risks, and the risks will only grow: twenty years from now, China will have a lot more missiles.

*

The drift to antagonism is already underway. For the last fifteen years China's massive defence build-up has been designed to counter American forces in the Western Pacific, and responding to China has driven America's air and naval programs. Since 2000 American diplomats have been laying the groundwork for a coalition to contain China in case it is needed, especially by courting Delhi as a counterbalance to Beijing. They have also been trying to build closer links among America's traditional allies in Asia through measures such as the US–Australia–Japan Trilateral

Strategic Dialogue. Meanwhile China is assertively, and often successfully, constraining US naval operations in the seas around Asia, as it did in August when protests from Beijing forced a US–South Korean exercise to be moved from the Yellow Sea to the Sea of Japan. That would simply not have happened a decade ago.

Meanwhile the global financial crisis has made Americans more aware of China's economic achievements, and more uneasy about their ability to compete. Many economists say that long-term solutions to America's economic problems require it to borrow less and produce more, especially in manufacturing. But how can America compete with China in manufacturing without driving wages down closer to Chinese levels? Anxieties like these contribute to a broader sense of antagonism; so do fears that China may be trying to lock up supplies of minerals and energy by investing in Africa and elsewhere.

Finally, there is fear of a looming ideological contest between Beijing's and Washington's political "models," reviving memories of the Cold War battle of ideas between communism and capitalism. America's problems have dented the assumption that their system provides the only viable model for a successful society in the twenty-first century, and China's success makes it the obvious alternative. It is unlikely to become a full-scale ideological struggle because, unlike the US and the Soviets, China has little desire to export its political system. China's exceptionalism is as strong as America's, but it is exclusive rather than evangelical. They believe their society is the best in the world, but they are in no hurry to persuade others to copy it, because they believe its strengths lie in things that are unique to China. So while Beijing is probably happy to see the gloss come off America's model, it will not crusade on behalf of its own. The fear that it might do so shows how readily people try to fit China into a pattern carried over from the Soviet Union and the Cold War. That is not helpful.

The news is not all bad. The day-to-day management of the American relationship with China remains quite good. Differences over Taiwan have been managed effectively for the past few years, helped by Taiwanese voters' rejection of the adventurous Democratic Progressive Party in favour of the Kuomintang's more accommodating approach to Beijing. Washington and Beijing have tactical differences over North Korea, but their strategic objectives are aligned, at least in the medium term. The Six-Party Talks have proved a welcome opportunity for them to explore what it would be like to work together as equals, and provide the best model we have of how a broader Concert of Asia might function. The two sides appear to avoid conflict in their complex and vital economic relationship reasonably well. And so far, when military incidents occur, such as China's harassment of a US Navy "research" ship near a major Chinese submarine base last year, they have been defused. It is probably a mistake to read too much into periodic rough patches in bilateral diplomacy, such as China's complaints about American arms sales to Taiwan, or American complaints about Chinese anti-satellite weapons testing.

It is the deeper trends we need to worry about. As China's power grows, the danger that it will overtake America will become clearer to Americans. If America's economic troubles deepen, it will be all the more natural to blame China. As Chinese leaders become more pushy, as they have so strikingly in the past year or two, Americans will feel more directly challenged and will be all the more inclined to push back. As China's military power grows, the urge for America to arm up in response will gather strength. As other countries accommodate themselves to China's power and try to profit from its growth, American diplomacy will become more determined to pull them back into America's fold. As Japan feels more pressured by China, it will urge America towards more assertive containment. The further all these trends progress, the harder it will be to change tack and seek some form of partnership.

None of this means eventual conflict between America and China is inevitable, but it is a real and very serious risk. It could happen quickly, and at any time, if the two powers are drawn into a military clash – over Taiwan or some other, perhaps trivial, incident that gets out of hand.

Or the drift to conflict could build slowly, as the trends we have identified gain momentum and a sense of inevitability sets in. I think this process is already underway, and it will continue unless somebody does something big to stop it.

QE 39 2010 **47**

Australia is a *status quo* power. We like the way Asia has worked until now. No other country in Asia – perhaps none in the world – has relied for so long, and so deeply, and so happily on America. None has benefited more from an alliance with that remarkable country. None has more cause to regret that its primacy in Asia may be passing. None needs more urgently to consider what we should do about it. And none of the alternatives on offer will be as good for us as the last forty years have been. If the age of uncontested American primacy is going to pass, we need to start thinking about which of the alternatives is best for us, and how we can get it.

Start with some basic principles. Australia wants peace and stability. We want the strongest possible economic relationship with China and the strongest possible strategic relationship with the US. We want the US engaged in the region and allied to Australia, and we want China to fulfil its potential as the economic powerhouse of the region and the locomotive for Australia's prosperity. These principles are important, but they leave all the hard questions unanswered. How much political and strategic power are we happy for China to have as the price for peace? How much power are we prepared to see the US concede? What kind of new order would suit us best? What can we do to help bring it about? How will we have to change to adapt to it? The best way to start answering these questions is to look at the implications for us of America's choices.

If the US withdraws from Asia, Australia will be left without a great and powerful friend for the first time in our history. Alliance loyalists might hope that the bonds of history, culture and values will keep America committed to our security even if it has abandoned strategic commitments elsewhere in Asia. Don't bet the country on it. Sentiment only goes so far in international affairs. America would have few hard interests in Australia if it were no longer trying to sustain a major role in Asia, so it would be unwise to expect Americans to commit real resources – financial, military or diplomatic – to protect us. America would no doubt remain a close friend, but not the kind of friend we believe it has been for seventy years now. More than ever before in our history, we would be on our own.

What that meant would depend on what happened in Asia as American engagement ebbed. As we have seen, it is unlikely but possible that Asia could accept China as a soft hegemon. If that happened, Australia would have little choice but to adapt to life in China's orbit. It would take a lot of getting used to, but geography would help – we are a long way from Beijing and might enjoy a little more room to manoeuvre than those closer to the centre of power. Compared to some of the possibilities, this is far from the worst future Australia might face. Even so, it would be very different from the world we have known. Since 1788 Australia has always enjoyed a very close and trusting relationship with the world's strongest power, and we just take that for granted. Living in China's orbit would introduce us to the pressures that most countries live with all the time, and our room to move would be severely constrained. Even under soft hegemony we would pay a high price for resisting Chinese pressure on any issue that mattered to them.

It is much more likely, however, that if America went home, Asia would be convulsed by rivalry among China, Japan and India. That could easily spill into our nearer neighbourhood as the great powers tried to expand their spheres of influence, and if so, it would stifle trade and other links. At worst, it could escalate into bitter, intense and protracted warfare among our most important trading partners, from which Australia could hardly escape unscathed even if we remained neutral. If this happens, Asia without America would be a lonelier, poorer and more dangerous place for Australia.

Australia would be much happier if America took the second option and decided to share power with China and the other major countries in a concert. In this scenario America would remain strongly engaged and would constrain China and the other strong countries from using their power too heavy-handedly. Australia could remain an American ally, and trade with China could flourish. But it would still be very different from the Asia we have known, and so too would our alliance with America. We could no longer assume that it would always put our interests ahead of everyone else's in Asia. To maintain a concert's delicate balance, each of the great powers must be very sensitive to the interests of the others. That means the interests of smaller countries, even when they are close allies, must take second place when there is a clash.

This would not just be a problem for Australia. The idea of the great powers getting together to run Asia among themselves would make a lot of other middle and small countries uneasy. They would no doubt prefer to see Asia's affairs managed by one or other of the region's many multi-lateral talkfests – APEC, ARF, EAS, ASEAN+3, even Kevin Rudd's APc – because they would get a seat at the table. Many Australians might agree. The problem is that the bigger any forum becomes, the less effective it is likely to be. There is no chance of negotiating Asia's new power balance with twenty or thirty countries at the table. Meetings like that are much more likely to display and deepen tensions than to resolve them. The deals to reduce tensions and accommodate conflicting ambitions will be done, if at all, bilaterally between the big states themselves. So middle and smaller powers have to choose between living with whatever deals the great powers strike among themselves, or accepting the consequences if the great powers fail to reach a deal and start fighting instead. This should be an easy choice to make. Much better to be locked out of the deals the great powers make to prevent conflict than to suffer the consequences if the deals aren't done.

Australia's early statesmen learned all this in the late nineteenth century, when Britain consistently overruled Australian concerns about foreign intrusions into the Southwest Pacific. Alfred Deakin and his colleagues discovered that, despite the ties of blood and empire, Whitehall would never risk irritating Germany or France – or later, Japan – just because Australia was worried that their Pacific colonies might be used as bases for attacks on us. Britain's overriding priority was to keep its relations with fellow members of the European concert stable: compared to that, our little local worries didn't rate. In retrospect the British were right.

We would find the same thing again if America joined a Concert of Asia. Washington's highest priority would be to keep relations with the other great powers on an even keel. As long as China and the others didn't breach the basic rules that held the concert together, America would be very reluctant to cross them on our behalf. That would leave China – or the other major powers – plenty of scope to lean on us, within limits. This means a concert of power in Asia would have both advantages and disadvantages for Australia. It would keep the peace among the major powers, which would allow us to keep trading with all of them and prevent us being drawn into their rivalries and conflicts. Our alliance with the US would survive, but the alliance would do less for us than it has in the past. We would be more on our own.

America's third option, competing with China, is darker than that, and the more intense the conflict, the darker it would grow. A sustained strategic struggle between the world's two strongest states would drive Asia's economy backwards, taking Australia's with it. It would divide the region into antagonistic camps and confront Australia with some very painful choices. As long as we remained committed to America, its commitment to us would remain strong, and the relationship would probably grow even closer. But the alliance would cost us a lot more and do much less for us than it has done for the past few decades.

*

Australia therefore faces big, hard choices whichever way Asia goes. It is some comfort to know that we have faced choices like this three times before in our history, and each time they were managed rather well. The first time was with the eclipse of British power in the late nineteenth century, which meant that we could no longer assume the Royal Navy would defend us just as Japan's power in Asia grew. In response the Australian colonies organised themselves into a federation so that they could better provide for their collective defence and improve their ability to influence British strategic decisions. Notwithstanding the tragedies of the two world wars, Australia remained secure and prosperous.

The second time was after World War II, when the European empires were swept from Asia. Australia suddenly found itself surrounded by newly independent nations, in the midst of a Cold War and no longer able to rely on Britain for much, if any, help. In response we converted our wartime partnership with America into a permanent alliance, accepted a share in protecting Western strategic interests in Southeast Asia, built new permanent armed forces and developed new forms of cooperation with our allies and neighbours. All this — what became known as "Forward Defence" — was designed to meet the new challenges by keeping our region peaceful and out of communist hands. Notwithstanding failure in Vietnam, it worked for Australia by helping to build the current order in Asia and establishing Australia's place in it.

Then, as failure in Vietnam loomed in the late 1960s, Australia seemed to face a third traumatic transformation. As we have seen, American power at that time appeared to be waning, China seemed to be gaining, Japan was restive and India showed growing potential. A new Asian power balance was apparently evolving, in which America would play a smaller role as it began to share power with the emerging Asian giants. It sounds familiar to us today. The difference is that forty years ago this prospect stimulated an intense and very fruitful debate, inside and outside government, about how Australia should respond. The debaters included Coral Bell, Hedley Bull, Donald Horne, Bruce Grant, Max Teichmann, Robert O'Neill, Tom Millar and Harry Gelber. It engaged all sides of politics, from B.A. Santamaria and Malcolm Fraser to Gough Whitlam, with all making important contributions. Meanwhile, in the bureaucracy new approaches were developed by Arthur Tange and the group of very talented people he nurtured in Defence, including Bob Hamilton and Bill Pritchett.

In the event, of course, things worked out differently. America recovered from Vietnam, and China still had a long way to go before it could challenge American power, as Mao realised when he made his deal with Nixon. But today the predictions of forty years ago appear not so much wrong as premature, and the ideas developed then seem relevant once more as we contemplate a new balance of power in Asia. Certainly, the debate they had then is the kind of debate we need now. They had an advantage over us, of course, because their thinking was nourished by the experience of the 1950s and 1960s – Malaya, Korea, West Papua, the Indonesia–Malaysia "Confrontation" and Vietnam, against the background of the Cold War at its worst – with World War II still a vivid memory for many.

Today we start thinking about Australia's strategic future from a very different, more innocent place. After forty years of peace in Asia, and twenty years after the Cold War, we do not have much experience of power politics, so we have to start almost from scratch.

First we must accept the unwelcome idea that power politics matters again. This means we should look at America, and China, and ourselves in new ways. Our debates about America need to get beyond "pro-American" versus "anti-American." It is not anti-American to recognise the implications of China's rise for America's role in Asia. It is not pro-American to argue that Australia's interests would be best served by America staying strategically engaged. It is not anti-American to say that they would not be best served by America competing with China for primacy. Ultimately, our deeper feelings towards America do not matter much: the alliance will only survive for as long as the US role in Asia serves our interests, and that is something we can no longer take for granted.

In the same way, our thinking about China needs to move beyond "pro" and "anti" labels. It is neither pro- nor anti-Chinese to recognise that China's power is growing. It is neither pro- nor anti-Chinese to consider what that means for Asia. It is neither pro- nor anti-Chinese to ask how Australia can best adapt to those changes. Learning to think straight about a powerful China will not be easy. The events we are living through challenge some very deep assumptions and attitudes in Western societies, including our own. We feel edgy – part disbelieving, part disapproving – at the idea that China could once more become the richest and strongest country on the globe. That is not the way we think the world works. Rather like China's mandarins confronting European power two centuries ago, we try to persuade ourselves that Western power will remain, if not greater, then at least more legitimate, than China's. Needless to say, that didn't work for the mandarins.

If we plan to get rich on China's growth, we had better get used to the idea of it as a very powerful state. That means getting used to the idea that there is nothing inherently illegitimate about China's power, nor about China using it to promote its interests. That is what strong states do. As we have seen, there need to be limits on how China uses its power, perhaps based on those set out in the Charter of the United Nations. But China will not accept any tighter limits than other countries – including the US – accept for themselves, and it is already too strong for us to enforce constraints on its power that it does not accept, other than at immense and tragic cost.

Australians still harbour a sense that we and our allies can set the terms of our relationship with China, as we have for two centuries past. As an outpost of the West, we see that as our birthright. But in future this will not be true. We will have to negotiate our relationship with China, and we have not quite got used to that idea. Because China's values are different from ours, we tend to see any compromise with Beijing as a sacrifice of our values on the altar of expediency. We will have to think our way through this, because we cannot learn to live with a powerful China if we regard every accommodation as a betrayal of principle.

China's growing power does not threaten Australia, but it does undermine the international order in Asia which has kept Australia safe and prosperous for a long time. Whether what follows is peaceful or turbulent does not just depend on China, but on all of us. We have to consider what we can do to bring about a good outcome and help prevent a bad one. This is important because there is a real chance of a bad outcome, which would see our international environment deteriorate sharply and quickly, with consequences for every aspect of our national life.

Australians have not faced a foreign-policy challenge like this for a long time, and we are out of practice. For decades our foreign policy has been modest, more concerned with helping other people deal with their problems than with managing our own. Now we face serious problems of our own, from which two tasks flow. First, to consider how we can best shape Asia's future order to suit our interests. Second, to consider how Australia can prepare for different outcomes, good or bad.

Shaping the future to suit us means, first, recognising the need for change. As Asia's strategic plates shift, trying to preserve the order that has worked so well for us until now might be worse than futile. None of Asia's probable futures will be as comfortable for us as the recent past, but some would be much better than others. The larger the role America plays in Asia, the better it will be for Australia, as long as that role is accepted rather than contested by the other major powers. That makes it clear that the best outcome for Australia would be for America to relinquish primacy and share power with China and the other major powers in a Concert of Asia. This is also the best outcome for the rest of Asia, and for America. But unfortunately it is the hardest to achieve, because each of the great powers has to give up so much to make it happen. As we have seen, it is particularly hard for America, because as the strongest power and the current leader, it has to begin the cycle of compromise if it is to gain momentum. That makes it clear what Australia should do. We should try to persuade America that it would be in everyone's best interests for it to relinquish primacy in Asia, but remain engaged as a member of a collective leadership – staying in Asia to balance, not to dominate.

It will not be easy. In fact, it is almost certainly the hardest diplomatic task Australia has ever contemplated. The basic argument is simple enough. The talking points would go something like this:

- China will probably keep growing, and if it does, uncontested US primacy becomes unsustainable;
- Strategic competition with China would be dangerous, costly and quite possibly unsuccessful;
- US withdrawal would destabilise the region;
- The best outcome for all would be for the US to lead Asia's transition to a collective leadership of great powers, based on the principles of the Charter of the United Nations;
- The sooner the US starts the better, because time is not on its side;
- Nothing is lost if China refuses to join, and the nature of its future intentions will have become clearer.

That is the easy part. The hard part would be presenting this argument in Washington and getting Americans to listen. It is not an argument that Americans want to hear. They are only just beginning to apprehend the scale of the challenge that China poses, and they are still a million miles from accepting that they should share power with China rather than compete with it. So this would be a difficult conversation; very different from the cosy chats that Australian leaders normally have with their American counterparts. However, it would not break the alliance and it might, in the long run, save it.

Many people might wonder whether it is even worth trying, because the chances of moving American opinion on this issue are so small. That may underestimate both us and the Americans. America remains a very receptive society, with an open market in ideas. It can be surprisingly easy to launch an idea and have it taken up and developed. To make an impact would require a sustained campaign both inside the US government and in the wider public arena. Who is better placed than Australia to make the argument to Americans? As its oldest and closest ally in Asia, we have better credentials in Washington than we probably deserve, and we should use them now when it really matters. Besides, what would we lose by trying?

We could give the broad message more bite by offering some specific ideas about how to move the US–China relationship in the right direction. One such idea concerns Taiwan. The US and China have managed the Taiwan issue quite well in recent years, but it remains a fundamental point of difference. The US could start to change that and lower the temperature over Taiwan by formally stating that it would actively support Taiwan's *eventual, peaceful, consensual* reunification with China. Perhaps surprisingly, America has never said such a thing before. A declaration along these lines would hardly give much away, because those three adjectives carry a lot of freight. If the Taiwanese people of their own volition decide they want to join the mainland on such a basis, why should the US object? And surely America loses nothing by conceding that it is possible the Taiwanese people might make such a choice. In fact, America's failure to make this kind of declaration until now leaves the suspicion that it would actively oppose reunification even if the people of Taiwan wanted it. So making it now would be an easy, low-cost, low-risk way to demonstrate acceptance and recognition of China's interests and its legitimacy.

The other idea concerns nuclear strategy. There is a real risk that fears about each other's nuclear forces could increase suspicion and hostility between America and China. China has very few weapons capable of hitting the US, but Beijing believes that it has sufficient to protect it from nuclear blackmail. However, there is a suspicion in China that America believes its much larger nuclear and conventional forces, plus its growing national missile defences, could destroy China's retaliatory forces and hence lay China open to American nuclear intimidation.

The Obama administration's recent Nuclear Posture Review did nothing to allay this concern. Like the Bush administration, it refuses to acknowledge China as a nuclear "peer" with whom it has a relationship of mutual nuclear deterrence. Inevitably, China is responding by building more missiles to preserve its ability to strike at the US. Inevitably, the US in turn sees this as threatening, and the risk is that it will redouble its efforts to neutralise China's deterrent.

The result is likely to be an escalating arms race, creating a spiral of distrust which could easily poison the wider relationship and increase the risk of nuclear war. There is a simple solution: the US and China could negotiate a nuclear arms-control agreement to prevent the race getting out of hand. The US would have to acknowledge China as a nuclear peer, forgoing any ambitions to use nuclear threats to intimidate Beijing. China would have to abandon its hopes to build a bigger and more flexible nuclear capability. In return, both stand to gain a more stable relationship with the other. Australia can help by advocating that Washington and Beijing should start to negotiate such an agreement.

The other way Australia could sharpen its message in Washington would be to get other Asian countries to join in. Everyone else in Asia – except Japan, as we have seen – is in the same boat. We all value America's role in Asia. We all want to avoid US–China conflict. We all want America to stay engaged to balance China, but none of us wants to see tension between them escalate. Australia should start talking to its neighbours, including Indonesia, South Korea, Singapore, India and even Japan, to encourage them to see the future our way and lend their weight to our diplomacy in Washington.

Finally, of course, we need to talk to China. China needs to be persuaded that it, too, should settle for a shared leadership in Asia, a continued strong role for America and growing roles for Japan and India. Selling this message in Beijing would be no easier than in Washington, but that is hardly a reason not to try.

First, however, before we start trying to persuade others about the best future for Asia, we need to have our own debate about it here in Australia. This will be difficult. The suggestion that we would urge the US to relinquish primacy in favour of shared leadership with China runs against our oldest and deepest foreign-policy principles. We have always believed that our security required the domination of the Western Pacific by an Anglo-Saxon maritime power, and we have always given priority to supporting our ally's primacy however and wherever we could. That instinct remains as strong today as ever. We can hardly imagine what it would be like to live in an Asia which is not led by the US. All our history and instincts therefore incline us to push the US to contest China's challenge and maintain the *status quo* for as long as possible. Yet our interests and our future should incline us to push the other way. We will need to sort this out among ourselves before we start talking to others about what to do. That means the first step in Australia's new strategic diplomacy is for our leaders to start explaining and debating the issues and options and solutions here at home. No one is doing that.

No matter what we say and do, there is a good chance that things will not go the way we would prefer. A decade or two from now, America could very easily be locked in a struggle with China for regional leadership, or slowly withdrawing from Asia. What would Australia do then? What are the options for Australia in circumstances so different from those we have known? These questions raise deep issues that we have not debated for a long time. They now loom, very important for our future, and quite urgent. Key decisions need to be made soon about Australia's role in this very different Asian century, because options will begin to close before long if we do not start to build the armed forces and diplomatic relations we could need.

In broad terms Australia has five alternatives in a more contested Asia. We can remain allied to America, seek another great and powerful friend, opt for armed neutrality, build a regional alliance with our Southeast Asian neighbours, or do nothing and hope for the best. We will explore each of them briefly in turn.

Our first option, of course, is to stick with the US. If the US stays to compete with China, this is Australia's default option – the one we end up taking if we cannot reach a clear decision to do something else. It has some attractions. The US will remain a very strong power, so it would still be able to offer us a lot of protection against China, or anyone else. Even if it loses sea control in the Western Pacific, America will be easily capable of defending Australia's air and sea approaches. It will also remain capable of deterring a Chinese nuclear attack on Australia for as long as Washington can persuade Beijing that it is liable to suffer a nuclear attack in return.

As we have seen, though, being an ally of America when America is contending with China would be very different from the alliance we have enjoyed over the past few decades. We have had an easy ride. We think of ourselves as a close and loyal ally of the US, but in fact the alliance costs us little. We have no US forces based here. None of our forces are permanently based overseas to support the US. The conditions under which we would support American forces in a major conflict are only vaguely delineated. Australian forces have little capacity to support America in a serious Asian war. All this would change if we remained a close American ally while America was perennially at risk of war with China. The more intense that risk became, the more America would demand of us, and if we cast our lot in with them, there would be no option but to comply. We would need to do whatever we could to make sure that they didn't abandon the contest and that they didn't lose it. We would also want to be able to influence America's decisions as much as possible, because these would be so critical for our future.

The costs would be enormous. In an intensifying conflict, our trade relationship with China would, of course, collapse, and relations else-where in Asia would become more complex. We would need to do more to support the US militarily, building bigger armed forces, hosting US bases and, if war came, sending big contingents of our armed forces to fight. The risk of being drawn into a major war with a nuclear-armed power would be much greater than ever before. We would end up less secure and less prosperous than we have been for several generations. And there would always be the further risk that the US, having stumbled into a strategic contest with China which it might not be able to win, could change its mind and withdraw to Hawaii, leaving us on China's side of the ocean without an ally.

This is not a good future for Australia. It is not the low-cost, low-risk US alliance we know and love. Sticking with the old alliance in new and different circumstances produces a very different and much less happy outcome. Many Australians will assume, however, that we would have no choice, because we have always depended on Britain or America as our great and powerful friend. But there are other options. None of them is very appealing, but we would be foolish to stick with the alliance and risk a drift into conflict without at least looking at the alternatives. And of course, if America withdraws from Asia, remaining a loyal ally would no longer be an option at all.

The first alternative would be for Australia to build a new alliance with a new "great and powerful friend." We have done this before: as British power faded through the last century, we switched allegiance to America. We could just repeat the manoeuvre and, as America is eclipsed, move on to find a new protector. There are some big questions, though. First, which great power would we choose? One obvious candidate is China itself. We have traditionally allied ourselves with the strongest power in Asia, so if China is going to be the strongest power, why not choose it? It sounds logical, but the closer you look, the less it appeals. If China became the dominant power in Asia, why would it want Australia as an ally? We would be subject to China's power whether we were an ally or not. An alliance with us would not help China much, so China would have little reason to help us against others, and the country we would have most to fear would be China itself. And could we trust China, in the way we have trusted Britain and America, never to use its power to our disadvantage? This is where the much-hyped links of history, values and culture really do make a difference. Could Australia ever trust any other country in this way? I do not think so.

The calculus would be different if China were only one of a number of great powers in Asia. If the next few decades see a strategic contest between China, Japan and India, then China might well look for allies, and Australia could be a useful addition to its team. But then we would encounter many of the same problems we would face as an American ally in a contested Asia, because China too would expect us to support it strongly against the other great powers, up to and including participation in a major war. Allying with any great power that is competing with other great powers is a dangerous and costly business. China might easily demand more of us than the US, and offer even less in return.

The same problems might discourage us from turning to India or Japan to replace America. In some ways they are better prospective allies than

China. They both seem less threatening, because they are democracies and because they are not as strong. They might welcome Australia as an ally if they were vying with China, and the more intense the rivalry, the more they might become committed to us. By the same token, though, the more intense the rivalry, the more they would expect of us, and the more costly and risky the alliance would be. The closer you look, the less appealing any of the alternative great-power allies appears. If we really want a great and powerful friend and America is still available, we'd be better off sticking with it than shopping around. If America is not available, we'd be better off looking for other options.

The natural alternative is to forget alliances altogether and opt for armed neutrality, like the Swiss and the Swedes. Such a model has obvious attractions for Australia. We have a continent of our own, far enough from the major powers to keep out of their way and protected by the sea. We could declare to the world that we will not align with anyone in Asia's strategic circus, and try to stay on reasonable terms with everyone. In the past this has often seemed an appealing idea to critics of the US alliance. However, armed neutrality in a contested Asia would be very different from going it alone in a stable Asia under US primacy. The more contested Asia becomes, the more seriously we would have to take the "armed" bit of armed neutrality. The Swiss and Swedes succeeded because their armed forces were big enough to make attacking them more trouble than it was worth, even for a major power. Australia might be able to build the forces to do that, but as we will see, it would be neither easy nor cheap.

Another issue is that our geostrategic situation is different from either Switzerland's or Sweden's in critical ways. Armed neutrality worked for them because their big neighbours were willing and able to fight to preserve the European order on which they depended. Neither of them had sufficient weight to affect the outcome of the conflicts in which their interests were so vitally engaged. That meant that whether or not they joined in the defence of Europe's order made little difference. Australia might not be in that position. If we had forces big enough to defend ourselves as an armed neutral, especially air and naval forces, then we would have forces big enough to make a real difference to a conflict in our maritime neighbourhood, even against a major power. In that case it would be bad strategic policy to hang back from a conflict in which the security of our neighbourhood was at stake, if by joining in we could tip the balance in a direction that kept us safe.

This suggests that instead of armed neutrality a better approach might be to team up with our middle-power neighbours in Southeast Asia. This is our fourth option. It too has a history: "regional defence" was one of the big ideas in the late '60s and early '70s before the post-Vietnam peace settled on Asia. It would not necessarily save us much defence effort compared to armed neutrality, because free-riding would not be an option. The security we would find in a regional alliance would depend absolutely on how much we contributed. We would have to matter to our allies if we wanted to be confident that they would take risks for us. That means having armed forces that could make a difference to outcomes and give us real influence on our allies' priorities.

Even so, a regional alliance could still offer big advantages over armed neutrality. Geographically the arguments are clear. The best way to defend Australia from any of Asia's major powers has always been to keep them out of the huge archipelago to our north, and hence out of range of Australia. Helping our neighbours defend their territory therefore looks a good way to get them to help defend ours. There has always been a question about how far north we should take this argument, but it makes sense to stay away from the Asian mainland and concentrate on the islands and peninsulas of maritime Southeast Asia: Malaysia, Singapore, perhaps the Philippines, the Melanesian islands and, of course, Indonesia. Indonesia is the big one here in every sense, and the credibility of a regional defence strategy for Australia hinges on whether it would play in Jakarta.

Indonesia occupies a unique place in Australian strategic calculations. It is our only close neighbour with any serious potential weight, which makes us inherently ambivalent about it. The stronger Indonesia becomes, the more it could threaten us, but equally the more it could help to protect us from others. That means we don't know whether to hope that it stays weak or grows strong. Whatever we hope for, there is a good chance that Indonesia, if it keeps its act together, will grow fast over the next few decades. If so, it will become a serious strategic player in Asia in its own right – not quite a great power, because its population is still much smaller than China's and India's, but a middle power of real weight. It will certainly be stronger than Australia, perhaps quite a lot stronger.

All this will change our relationship with Indonesia completely. The stronger it becomes, the more important a stable and cooperative relationship with Jakarta will be for Australia. The more contested Asia becomes, the more important Indonesia will be as a potential ally. Without Indonesia, the idea of a regional alliance in maritime Southeast Asia would go nowhere. With Indonesia, it could have a real chance, and might offer Australia the best way to avoid entanglement in Asian major-power rivalries without finding ourselves all alone. Together, Indonesia and Australia would be quite formidable, as we neatly complement each other's strengths. But none of this is possible unless we can build a bilateral relationship with Indonesia that overcomes the suspicions and grievances on both sides. From Australia's side that raises big questions. Just as China's rise challenges some deep preconceptions, Australia has hardly begun to come to terms with the probability that our close neighbour may soon be a strong country, and very important to us in the decades ahead on issues much more significant than people-smuggling.

If this looks too hard, Australia's final option would be to opt out and drift towards unarmed neutrality – what we might call the New Zealand option. Australians tend to laugh at this idea, but we should hold back our giggles until we understand the alternatives better and are sure we are willing to pay what they would cost. The four options we have considered so far would all require Australia to spend much more on defence and build much more capable armed forces, either to pull our weight in an alliance or to stand alone. Except for armed neutrality, they also involve the risk of being dragged into conflicts we would rather avoid. We could instead, like New Zealand, simply rely on neutrality and remoteness to keep us clear of Asia's turmoils, and hope they keep away from us. This is a serious possibility, either as a deliberate and considered choice, or because we might simply fail to do what is necessary to avoid it.

We might deliberately choose this option if the costs of the alternatives seem out of proportion to the risks we face. New Zealand's defence policy is based on just this calculation. To New Zealanders, the risk of direct attack seems very low, and the forces they would need in order to contribute anything substantial to regional defence would cost a very big slice of their relatively small economy. So they have decided, on balance, to live with the risk and spend the money on other things. There is nothing inherently wrong with this calculation. Every country's defence policy strikes some balance between cost and risk, and all of us live with risks that seem too remote to justify the costs of addressing them. This is as true of Australia as anyone – there are many threats that the Australian defence force today cannot protect us from, but we accept that, because the risks seem low and the costs would be high.

If Asia becomes more contested over the next few decades, Australia will need to reassess both sides of this ledger. Obviously our risks may go up, but by how much? Many people would wonder why strategic competition between the US and China, or between China and Japan, need involve us. And why would anyone attack Australia directly? For decades it has been hard to imagine Australia coming under direct attack; would that necessarily change much in a more contested Asia? On the other side of the ledger, Australia would need to spend a lot more money to build forces that could defend the continent alone or to contribute substantially to a regional or great-power alliance. When the costs are high and the risks seem low, it is easy to see the merits of the New Zealand solution.

It all depends on how high the costs really are, and how low the risks turn out to be. On the risk side, we cannot assume our future will be as secure as the past few decades. We could possibly avoid being drawn into distant major-power confrontations by remaining unaligned, but we could not be at all sure that their confrontations would not come to us. There is a real chance that their antagonism would show up in maritime Southeast Asia, and even in the South Pacific, as different sides tried to build spheres of influence. To some degree that is already happening, and it is easy enough to construct scenarios in which this escalates and Australia again finds major-power conflict on our doorstep, as we did in 1942.

Finally, of course, we are different from New Zealand, because New Zealand has Australia. Their strategic calculations depend on Australia's strength to reduce their risks. If we had a close, culturally connected neighbour between us and Asia, four times our size and with more than four times our wealth, as they do, we would have a defence policy much more like New Zealand's. But we don't, which means we should think carefully before choosing unarmed neutrality. We should also watch out that we don't wake up one day to find that we have slid into unarmed neutrality without noticing. It would be easy to do. All the alternative options require real effort, building new alliances or much more capable armed forces or both. Unless we decide to make that effort, we will find ourselves following New Zealand's example by default.

*

The difference we see between ourselves and New Zealand is that we are a middle power and they are a small power. The big strategic question for Australia today is whether we will make the effort to remain a middle power in the Asian century or resign ourselves to becoming a small power. Middle powers have enough weight to influence what happens around them so as to protect their interests. They can negotiate with great powers, not simply obey them. Small powers just take what happens. Most countries in the world are small powers. Only a couple of dozen at most can do much to shape the world around them. On the basic indices of power, we should be one of them – around fourteenth in the world in GDP and defence spending. We certainly speak of ourselves as a middle power – remember Kevin Rudd's "activist middle-power diplomacy"? – and we confidently envisage remaining one, as the 2009 Defence White Paper repeatedly reminded us.

But are we really a middle power today? No one should forget that our big successes – such as East Timor in 1999 – were only possible because we were backed by American power. Diplomatically, American power has made the international system work in our favour for a long time now. It is hard to remember when we last tried to make anything important happen internationally without America's support or at least its acquiescence – and that doesn't count. Being a middle power means being able to do things that a great power doesn't agree with, or even opposes, without the backing of another great power. It is hard to imagine us, if we faced a real test, doing that today.

Militarily, the key benchmark of middle power for Australia is the ability to defend the continent alone against a major Asian power. At first glance that seems impossible, but it might not be as hard as all that. It is not a matter of being able to defeat a major power like China in an all-out war. The question is whether we could raise the costs and risks of penetrating Australia's air and sea approaches to the point where a major power decided that it was not worth its while. Three factors would work to our advantage in doing this. First, we can assume that attacking Australia would never be a very high priority for a major power – our remoteness alone gives us some assurance of that – and that cuts down the costs we would need to impose to dissuade them. Second, a major power could only ever commit a small proportion of its total forces to penetrating our approaches unless it already dominated the rest of Asia, in which case we are in trouble. Third, we have a big operational advantage. We have only to deny our maritime approaches to an adversary, whereas it has to control them. The adversary's task is much harder than ours.

Even so, it is far from clear that we could do it. To be fair, this is not surprising, because we have not even thought of doing anything like this for the past forty years. The "defence self-reliance" we have proclaimed since the mid-1970s has always been limited to dealing with the kinds of threats that could emerge within the US-led order, and that ruled out any thought that we might have to deal with a major Asian power alone. Only in the 2000 White Paper did the government start to ask whether Australia might have to deal with this kind of risk unassisted. Alas, defence policy debate was soon hijacked by the War on Terror. Kevin Rudd's 2009 Defence White Paper reinstated the issue at the top of the agenda, only to decide that we had nothing to worry about for a couple of decades at least, and to defer any serious analysis, let alone any real decisions.

We might not have a couple of decades. Military capabilities take a long time to build. If Australia is to have the forces to be a middle power in a more contested Asia in 2040, decisions about what capabilities we need to build or buy must be made in the next few years. There is a lot to consider before those decisions can be made. We would need to determine our strategic objectives, which in turn would depend on our preferences among the five options sketched above. Then we need to analyse what kinds of military operations could most effectively achieve those objectives, what kinds of forces could most effectively perform them, whether we have the capacity to build and operate these forces, and how much it would all cost.

Australia cannot make any of these decisions, let alone implement them, without a much more serious approach to defence policy than any Australian government has taken for a generation. We have not taken defence seriously because any threat has seemed so unlikely and American support has been so certain. The result is a defence organisation – military and civilian – which can scarcely maintain and deliver many of the capabilities we have now, let alone plan and build the forces to make Australia a middle power in the Asian century. This is ultimately a failure of political leadership. Until political leaders take responsibility for making the big policy decisions to transform our defence organisation radically, there is no chance Australia will have the military weight to be a middle power in a few decades. We will be heading New Zealand's way whether we like it or not.

Today Australia spends a little under 2 per cent of its GDP on defence – about $1200 a year for each of us. A lot of that money is wasted, not just on doing things inefficiently, but by building and maintaining capabilities that we do not really need. However, even if we spent every dollar as efficiently as possible, 2 per cent would still not get us the forces to make us a middle power. Three per cent might just get us over the threshold, if it was spent very wisely indeed. We have not spent that much on defence since the early 1970s, when Asia's peaceful era began – which is not a coincidence. From 1950 to 1970, when the risks to our security seemed higher, we spent an average of more than 3.2 per cent. It would be perfectly possible for Australia to go back to this level of spending if the risks seemed to warrant it, but it would not be a step to be taken lightly.

And it would all come down to money in the end. Three per cent might not be enough, or it might not be enough for long, because the long-term trends are against us. The productivity revolution that is transforming China and reordering the world is changing our place in the world too, and especially our place in Asia. We are in relative decline, just as much as America is. Only twenty years ago Australia's economy was as big as China's, bigger than India's, and bigger than the whole of the Association of Southeast Asian Nations put together. Since then our economy has performed very well, but the tides of history are running against us. Today China's economy is four times the size of ours. Mark Thomson of the Australian Strategic Policy Institute calculates that by 2030 it will be nine times the size of ours, and by 2050, twenty times.

That makes you think. Nonetheless, I do not believe that Australia should abandon the aim of being a middle power in the Asian century before we have understood better what it would cost to achieve it, and what it would cost to let it go. Nor should we resign ourselves to sleep-walking into a role of timid automatism in an uncertain, contested Asia until we have done much more to understand how our region can remain peaceful and stable, and how we can help to bring that about. First, we need to accept that if China keeps growing, and it probably will, Asia will change. For Australia, foreign affairs and defence policy are getting serious again.

SOURCES

2.   Tony Abbott, *Battlelines*, Melbourne University Press, Melbourne, 2009, p. 160.

3.   "It seemed that Asia was headed for an even more dangerous era": see, for example, Hedley Bull, "The New Balance of Power in Asia and the Pacific," *Foreign Affairs*, Vol. 49, No. 4, July 1971.

4.   "in 1972 and cut a deal with Mao": The story of the visit is wonderfully told by Margaret MacMillan in *Nixon and Mao: The Week that Changed the World*, Random House, New York, 2007.

7.   "Howard was not expecting this when he took office": Howard's complex approach to China is described in Paul Kelly, *The March of Patriots*, Melbourne University Press, Melbourne, 2009.

8.   "Our aim is to see calm and constructive dialogue": Hansard, 24 October 2003, available at <www.aph.gov.au/hansard/reps/dailys/dr241003.pdf>.

12. "Many Chinese realised that to compete with the West": the story of China's long journey back to power is well told by Jonathan Fenby in *The Penguin History of Modern China: The Fall and Rise of a Great Power, 1859–2008*, Allen Lane, London; New York, 2008.

13. "Sceptics about China's future doubt it": see, for example, John Lee, *Will China Fail? The Limits and Contradictions of Market Socialism*, Centre for Independent Studies, Sydney, 2007.

14. "reaching the top of the economic table in the next few decades": the long-term demographic and economic trends are described in Mark Thomson, *The Human Tide: An Australian Perspective on Demographics and Security*, Australian Strategic Policy Institute, Barton, ACT, 2009.

15. "China's ruling party is much more Leninist than communist": Richard McGregor has recently written an excellent book on all this, *The Party: The Secret World of China's Communist Rulers*, Allen Lane, London, 2010.

21. "we can know something about their aspirations and their circumstances": my analysis of China's options, and of America's later in the essay, has been informed by a recent Lowy Institute publication by Malcolm Cook, Raoul Heinrichs, Rory Medcalf and Andrew Shearer, *Power and Choice: Asian Security Futures*, which is available at <www.lowyinstitute.org/AsiaSecurityProject.asp>.

29. "America can no longer assume that it has sea control in the Western Pacific": US Secretary of Defense Robert Gates went a long way towards acknowledging this in a speech earlier this year when he said, "The US will also face increasingly sophisticated underwater combat systems – including numbers of stealthy subs – all of which could end the operational sanctuary our Navy has enjoyed

in the Western Pacific for the better part of six decades." Available at <www. defense.gov/speeches/speech.aspx?speechid=1460>.

33. "A great deal has been written in America about China's rise": for example, in 2008 the US government itself published a report titled *Global Trends 2025: A Transformed World*. Available at <www.dni.gov/nic/NIC_2025_project.html>.

35. "the nation that I am most interested in building is our own": "Remarks by the President in Address to the Nation on the Way Forward in Afghanistan and Pakistan," speech at West Point Military Academy, New York, 1 December 2009. Available at <www.whitehouse.gov/the-press-office/remarks-president-address-nation-way-forward-afghanistan-and-pakistan>.

39. "this might be to misinterpret the lesson of Munich": Paul Kennedy has recently written about this question and its relevance to our approach to China in "A Time to Appease," *National Interest Online*, 22 June 2010. Available at <www.nationalinterest.org/Article.aspx?id=23542>.

43. "The issue of Soviet–American relations is in essence": from George Kennan, "The Sources of Soviet Conduct," *Foreign Affairs*, July 1947. Available at <www. historyguide.org/europe/kennan.html>.

57. "acceptance and recognition of China's interests and its legitimacy": I have more fully developed this idea in "The US, Taiwan and the PRC – Managing China's Rise: Policy Options for Australia," Melbourne Asia Policy Paper No. 5, November 2004. Available at <www.asialink.unimelb.edu.au/__data/assets/pdf_ file/0003/4197/mapp5.pdf>.

58. "Washington and Beijing should start to negotiate such an agreement": I have more fully developed this idea in "Stopping a Nuclear Arms Race Between the US and China," Lowy Institute for International Policy, August 2007. Available at <www.lowyinstitute.org/Publication.asp?pid=654>.

60. "Australia has five alternatives in a more contested Asia": a similar analysis of Australia's foreign-policy options was offered by Hedley Bull in his essay "Options for Australia," in Gordon McCarthy, ed., *Foreign Policy for Australia: Choices for the Seventies*, Angus and Robertson, Sydney, 1973.

62. "turning to India or Japan to replace America": Humphrey McQueen explored the idea of Japan as a new great and powerful friend for Australia in a different context in *Japan to the Rescue: Australian Security Around the Indonesian Archipelago During the American Century*, William Heinemann Australia, Melbourne, 1991.

63. "opt for armed neutrality, like the Swiss and the Swedes": the idea of armed neutrality as an alternative to alliance with the US in the Cold War was explored by David Martin in *Armed Neutrality for Australia*, Dove Communications, Melbourne, 1984; and by Max Teichmann in the 1970s.

Among the books I have found most useful on the issues considered in this essay are:

Andrew J. Bacevich, *The Limits of Power: The End of American Exceptionalism*, Black Inc., Melbourne, 2008.

Coral Bell, *The End of the Vasco da Gama Era*, Lowy Institute, Sydney, 2007. Available at <www.lowyinstitute.org/Publication.asp?pid=723>.

Bill Emmott, *Rivals: How the Power Struggle Between China, India and Japan Will Shape Our Next Decade*, Houghton Mifflin Harcourt, London; New York, 2008.

Harry G. Gelber, *The Dragon and the Foreign Devils: China and the World, 1100 BC to the Present*, Walker & Company, New York, 2007.

Stuart Harris, *Will China Divide Australia and the US?*, Australian Centre for American Studies, Sydney, 1998.

David L. Shambaugh (ed.), *Power Shift: China and Asia's New Dynamics*, University of California Press, Berkeley; London, 2005.

Patrick Tyler, *A Great Wall: Six Presidents and China*, PublicAffairs, New York, 1999.

Laura Tingle

There are worlds out there that some of us don't even know exist. One of them is called Doha. Doha is the current negotiation round of the World Trade Organisation, which commenced in November 2001. As Wikipedia notes, its objective is to lower trade barriers around the world, which allows countries to increase trade globally.

It has been stalled since 2008. And if ever there was a process stultifying in its bureaucracy and lack of progress, this would have to be it. When a colleague at the *Australian Financial Review* who was a Doha specialist left last year, we rather unkindly read out her first story for the paper in 2005 – which reported business alarm at the lack of Doha progress – and then read out her last story, which was almost identical.

Yet there are hundreds, perhaps thousands, of bureaucrats and politicians around the world who attend countless meetings about Doha every year. One such meeting took place in 2009. Australian representatives were there, but at a crucial point in the talks they informed their counterparts from other countries that they were sorry, but they were awaiting instructions from Canberra and would have to delay the talks for a while.

Word emerged that the reason for this was that the prime minister had been reading through the meeting agenda and thought he had a solution to finding a special trade instrument to solve one of the deadlocks in the discussions. Hours passed. My recollection of the story is that perhaps even a day or two passed.

All the delegates waited. Nothing happened. Finally, a call was made to the prime minister's office to find out what was happening.

Oh, turns out he'd thought about it but didn't have a solution after all.

A shame no one bothered to ring to say so.

Why a prime minister would bother himself with such minutiae is a mystery to most of us. But if you asked almost anybody in Canberra, stories like this about Kevin Rudd would surprise no one.

In the ruptured space left by his dramatically curtailed prime ministership, everyone is now coming out with such stories. And particularly amid the internecine warfare that has broken out as I write this piece in the first week of the election campaign, the forces that unseated Rudd are doing everything they can to demonise him to ensure he never comes back to be a pest as foreign minister.

I think often of the Doha story because it captures all the elements of the Kevin Rudd story that we have tried to come to terms with in the past three years: the vast scope of his intellectual policy nosiness; his perky determination to think that he alone can find a solution to something no one else has managed; his apparent obliviousness to the impact of his actions on other people.

I thought of it again as I stood in the freezing cold prime-ministerial courtyard on the morning of 24 June listening to Rudd outline the astonishingly long list of things his government had got done – or got started – of which he was proud.

I say "listening" advisedly. Crowds of Greek-chorus proportions tend to congregate around Parliament House on days like 24 June, and I spent that long, excruciating time staring into the large pink handbag of a rather glamorous – and tall – creature standing in front of me. Marooned behind the pink handbag, I found that those moments when a controlled, on-message Kevin Rudd kept almost losing it came out as terribly long, agonising silences, which only increased the sense of loneliness. I couldn't see that he was surrounded by his family, who were willing him through such a difficult time.

David Marr captured all this restless intellectual energy, its chaotic after-effects and Rudd's strange dealings with the rest of the human race in his *Quarterly Essay* on the political journey of Kevin Rudd.

It is a shame that so much of the reaction to Marr's wonderfully written piece focused on "the anger question," particularly as so much of the reaction misconstrued the point Marr made about that anger: not so much that Rudd is an angry man, but that anger at what he had witnessed in his life had shaped so much of his political agenda.

Having said that, I don't know whether I would use anger to explain what makes Kevin Rudd tick. That's not because I disagree with Marr's assessment, but because Rudd remains such a mystery to me, despite having dealt with him personally since the days of COAG meetings and the Goss government.

Marr's wonderful description of standing amid the euphoria of Suncorp Stadium on election night 2007 and of the new prime minister-elect completely missing the mood of the moment in his victory speech sums up so much about the former prime minister.

It is hard sometimes to avoid the impression that Rudd doesn't respond to people spontaneously but rather intellectualises what it is they might expect of him and what he wants from them. A Labor MP – one of the many who had just had enough of their prime minister by 23 June – told me a few days before Julia Gillard's coup that he had finally got in to see the prime minister after months of trying. Kevin was charming and funny, as he can be. But the MP found himself thinking, I am being managed here.

Rudd often gave people that same impression of calculation in other ways, such as in the story Marr tells of the former prime minister talking about "those Chinese fuckers rat-fucking us." There is something in the way Kevin Rudd swears which makes you think he feels he has to do it – that it is expected of him.

It was Paul Keating who said of Rudd that he was Labor, but not tribal Labor. Perhaps that is why his intellect told him, when confronted with the party machine – once he was in a position of power – that the way to treat the party was to treat it mean. That's what the machine and the party would expect.

One of the stories that emerged in the wake of the coup told how the Victorian senator David Feeney and others had gone in a delegation to complain about cutbacks in MPs' printing allowances.

Rudd reportedly told the delegation: "I don't care what you fuckers think!" He reportedly singled out Senator Feeney with, "You can get fucked."

Now, frankly, printing allowances are an outrage that have been used for years by both sides of politics to fund their safe-seat campaigns, and one of those good things Kevin Rudd – and John Faulkner as special minister of state – did was to cut these allowances back. So I'm sort of with Rudd on this. But was it necessary to show he was in control? Perhaps not.

When I was writing a profile in 2008 on the way Kevin Rudd ran his government, someone told me that Rudd relied on Wayne Swan for assessments of people because he had no real feel for them himself. Perhaps Swan's preparedness to help eventually peeled away.

For me it is the strange and lonely disconnection from so many of his colleagues that is the real mystery of the former prime minister – and of course it is the thing that brought him undone. A frontbencher said to me as the 2010 election campaign began, "Laura, just remember it wasn't the polls that were the reason Kevin was done over. It wasn't because we were worried that he would lose. It was that we were worried he might win and then we'd be stuck with him!"

Yet for all the complaints, Labor's first few weeks of Rudd-less government have had it showing just why he was able to develop such a dominant grip on power. Labor goes into the campaign a shallow, timid outfit that doesn't seem to know what it wants to do, except win, and not all that competent at putting in place the policies to achieve this.

Laura Tingle

Chris Uhlmann

In 2004 a senior Labor staffer was captivated by the withering opening paragraph on Billy McMahon in Paul Hasluck's book *The Chance of Politics*:

> I confess to a dislike of McMahon. The longer one is associated with him the deeper the contempt for him grows and I find it hard to allow him any merit. Disloyal, devious, dishonest, untrustworthy, petty, cowardly – all these adjectives have been weighed by me and I could not in truth modify or reduce any one of them in its application to him.

The staffer copied it and circulated it among some in the party with the question, "Who does this remind you of?"

He says the almost universal answer was, "Kevin Rudd."

In the end what is astonishing about Rudd is not that he fell so brutally, it is that he rose at all. His rise is a tribute to his great gifts: his intellect and unwavering determination to succeed in the face of scant enthusiasm for his cause inside caucus. His fall is due to his large flaws and the chaos these engendered in his office and government.

Rudd is a study in contrasts, with the capacity for great generosity of spirit and small acts of meanness. Above all he was an exemplar of the gulf between intelligence and wisdom. David Marr's timely and incisive essay details Rudd's enormous capacity to absorb and tediously regurgitate information, and his inability to distill and transform it. He quotes a staffer as saying, "For all the effort he doesn't come up with particularly interesting solutions to problems."

This combination of great detail coupled with shallow analysis is evident in Rudd's essays in the *Monthly* on religion and the financial crisis. The 2006 "Faith in Politics" essay set a high bar for the way a Christian should act in the world.

Rudd's model was the German theologian Dietrich Bonhoeffer, who demanded that injustice be confronted. Bonhoeffer asked, "Who speaks boldly to the state for those who cannot speak for themselves?" Rudd argued Christianity "must always take the side of the marginalised, the vulnerable and the oppressed."

But the real purpose of the essay was political: to compare this kind of faith, his faith, with that of John Howard, and to find his opponent wanting. He was recruiting Bonhoeffer to his cause and that put high words to a low purpose.

He found another recruit in the financial crisis. In his 2009 essay on it he wrote:

> The time has come, off the back of the current crisis, to proclaim that the great neo-liberal experiment of the past 30 years has failed, that the emperor has no clothes. Neo-liberalism and the free-market fundamentalism it has produced has been revealed as little more than personal greed dressed up as an economic philosophy. And, ironically, it now falls to social democracy to prevent liberal capitalism from cannibalising itself.

But this was sophistry dressed up as analysis. The purpose of the essay was to consign the Coalition to political history and claim that the only valid form of government for the foreseeable future was his.

The essay excluded many inconvenient truths. Bill Clinton, Bob Hawke and Paul Keating were all part of "the great neo-liberal experiment of the past 30 years," yet their role was airbrushed. As was the fact that the experiment has, largely, been a success in Australia. And how could a China expert write 7000 words on the global financial crisis and not mention the distortions caused by the rise of China and its fixed exchange rate?

Rudd cast himself as a philosopher king and was given to cloaking political arguments in moral garments. He called climate change "the great moral challenge of our generation." The financial crisis was not just a market failure but "a fundamental failure of values." So to disagree with this prime minister was not just to espouse bad policy, it was to be a bad person.

Yet if you lay down moral arguments like mines to blow up your opponents, you run the risk of stepping on one yourself. And when Rudd backed away from his government's response to climate change, he was mortally wounded in the minefield of his own rhetoric.

David Marr concludes that anger is "the juice in the machine" and that Rudd is a man "with rage at his core, impatient rage." I can't see into his heart, so it is impossible to know if this is true. He certainly had a temper, but many driven people do. We can only judge him by his words and actions and I think it is true to say that he was torn apart by the contradictions at his core.

In October 2009 I received an email from the *Australian*'s Cameron Stewart. He was writing a feature on the way Rudd governed, at a time when he was still wildly popular. He asked how Rudd was viewed, so I called some bureaucrats and Labor MPs and senators. The results of that straw poll were published in the *Weekend Australian Magazine* in November 2009.

> There is a view that [Rudd] has the face and bearing of a parson, and the heart and soul of a dictator. He has cowed his party, his caucus, his cabinet and the bureaucracy. He holds all the prizes, and anyone who wants to advance must pay homage to him. He bludgeons alternative opinions to death, and rules his own by both terrorising them and uniting them by kicking a hopeless foe that cannot wound him.
>
> He survives because he has been on the right side of every argument for the last two years and is a much better politician than anyone imagined. And they say when he falls – probably a very long time from now – it will be with blinding speed as his own party rushes to tear down his statue.

The end came more swiftly than any imagined. But it was always going to end this way.

Chris Uhlmann

Annabel Crabb

What would a normal person do, after being tipped out of his job, deserted by his colleagues and forced to relinquish his life's dream, all in the space of a few days and with the hardest bits broadcast live to a global television audience?

What would *you* do?

Normal answers to this question might include: Fall apart. Clean the house. Experiment with brandy-for-breakfast. Consider buying something off Demtel. Send forty-eight unsolicited pizzas to the home address of your principal oppressor.

Normal answers to this question do not include: Attend Question Time. Commence a campaign to be appointed Australian foreign minister. Jump on a plane bound for the Australian American Leadership Dialogue. Stage a grip-and-grin with Ban Ki-moon.

As David Marr demonstrates in his *Quarterly Essay*, Kevin Rudd does not answer to the same gods as ordinary humans. Marr's subject was Rudd's atypical relationship with power, but we can learn as much from the former prime minister's relinquishment of power as we did from watching him exert it. The same themes dominate: Utter indefatigability. Physical stamina. A certain robotic imperviousness to the reality at hand. A calm conviction, on the part of the subject, of his natural centrality to events.

My favourite bit in Marr's essay is not the celebrated "rage" thesis; nor is it any of the essay's enlightening material concerning Mr Rudd's past professional endeavours. My favourite passage is on page nineteen, and it goes like this:

> Marge Rudd drove him more than a thousand miles that year to speak. Eliminated in May from the Lions Club's "Youth of the Year Quest" in Brisbane, he then triumphed in the Jaycees' "Youth Speaks for Australia" competition, winning watches, sets of encyclopaedias,

a pile of books on ancient history for the school library and praise from the *Chronicle*: "Once again it's well done Kevin." After the local finals in tiny Biloela and the state finals at Clifton, he flew over to Perth a few weeks after his seventeenth birthday and lost. How did he respond to defeat? "He'd studied Caesar's troubles in the Gallic wars," says [former teacher] Fae Barber laconically. "It stood him in good stead."

This passage tells you just about all you need to know about congenital Rudd-ism. There's something about Marr's account of that juvenile oratory crusade that is priceless; perhaps it is the mental image of a young Kevin in pressed shorts grimly accumulating volumes of the *Encyclopaedia Britannica*, perhaps it is the exquisitely resigned tone of that "Once again it's well done Kevin" headline from the *Chronicle*.

To read it is to picture, irresistibly, the *Chronicle*'s editor; a middle-aged bloke, one assumes, trying stolidly to collate livestock prices while weathering serial visits from Kevin, armed with important messages about the Gallic wars.

That editor, anonymous to us now, was the first of many editors to experience the rare comet that was – is – Kevin Rudd. One hopes that the young Rudd's philosophical identification with the trials of Caesar has survived into middle age.

Whatever you think of the man – and the people paid to monitor this stuff reliably report that millions of Australians who liked Kevin07 as recently as a year ago could not bear him by April this year – you can't help but marvel at the brutality of the execution.

One is amply persuaded, not least by Marr's essay, that Kevin Rudd in office tended to be high-handed and isolationist; convinced, to an extent that proved fatal to the establishment of any sort of properly productive Cabinet, that he and only he could be trusted to make decisions of moment.

And there is little doubt that Mr Rudd's solution to the problem of climate change – "the greatest moral challenge of our time" – was so ensnarled by compromise when it surfaced as to be nearly unrecognisable from the clean lines of his campaign rhetoric.

But consider the mechanics of Mr Rudd's ousting. Electoral forensics trace the collapse in the former prime minister's public support back to April, when his government's decision to abandon its emissions trading scheme was first telegraphed to the Australian people by way of a leak to the *Sydney Morning Herald*.

We know now that this decision was one against which Mr Rudd had been holding out internally ever since the failed Copenhagen talks, in the face of strong pressure from his deputy, Julia Gillard, and his treasurer, Wayne Swan. Having succumbed to them and relinquished the emissions trading scheme, Mr Rudd's public standing then eroded to the point at which it became Julia Gillard's lugubrious duty to assassinate him.

The above is a simplistic view, of course; it's always more complicated than that. But you can sort of understand why Mr Rudd might be annoyed.

In the unfairly intimate glimpse the nation was afforded of Kevin Rudd on the day of his dethronement, it became clear exactly where the warmth in his life comes from. Not from his colleagues, barely any of whom bestirred themselves even to pretend to regret his passing, but from his sensible wife, Thérèse Rein, and three unnervingly normal offspring, who gathered about him with every appearance of good humour despite the dreadful circumstances.

How were the colleagues so completely estranged from the man who so recently won them a strong election result? Marr's essay gives us a lot of good pointers here. As a prime minister, Mr Rudd was not especially available to his comrades. And some of his decisions actively estranged them, like the decision to reduce their allowances and the repeated appointment of Liberals to high-profile jobs.

These gave offence, not so much because of the money involved (although, of course, that was a factor) but because they gave the impression that the Labor leader was more anxious to align himself with commonly held prejudices (politicians have all got their snouts in the trough) than he was to stand his ground and defend his colleagues.

In his own way, Kevin Rudd created in the minds of his MPs the same impression that Coalition MPs had of Malcolm Turnbull towards the end of his leadership: that their leader put his own interests before those of the party as a whole.

Annabel Crabb

Kerryn Goldsworthy

Reading David Marr's essay on Kevin Rudd in the wake of the events that saw Julia Gillard become prime minister on 24 June, it's now even more difficult than it was at the time to see why, in the days following its publication and despite a lot of positive feedback, the essay also got such a bad reaction from certain quarters of the commentariat both online and off.

Apart from the usual assortment of misreadings and misrepresentations, three things about the negative reactions were particularly odd. There was the criticism that Marr's essay, in hypothesising about Rudd's motivations and their roots in his childhood, was somehow not proper journalism. There was the almost exclusive concentration on what was actually a coda, an after-the-fact personal revelation taking up four paragraphs of the essay's eighty-six pages, about anger as the driving force of Rudd's personality. And there were the scornful objections, in which could sometimes be discerned a kind of repressed hysteria, to *any* discussion of people in general and of Rudd in particular that ventured into the territory of the psychological.

The first of these three things rests on a basic category mistake. Marr was not, in this instance, writing "journalism": he was writing an *essay*, a genre characterised chiefly by the elasticity of its definitional boundaries. The word comes from the French verb *essayer*, to try: an essay is an investigation, a foray, a "try" at a subject. It can be and often is an expedition into the unknown and, frequently, the unverifiable: memories; theories; hitherto unexplored veins of subject matter or uninhabited points of view. In fact, given the large amount of verifiable fact and the only occasional appearance of an identifiably personal voice, Marr's essay is well up the "journalism" end of the spectrum.

Furthermore, and again this is a matter of genre, those who criticised Marr for being "only" a journalist who had somehow strayed off his own professional patch were clearly not aware that he is also an experienced and gifted biographer, an expert in that genre where the exploration of the subject's childhood and the making of connections between childhood experience and adult life is one of the central points of the exercise. A biographical study seeks to make sense of the narrative of a life by finding patterns of cause and effect.

Secondly, there was the observation, made at the very end of the essay though foreshadowed at strategic points along the way, that in Marr's view the driving force of the "real" Kevin Rudd is anger: Marr describes having seen Rudd transformed by this emotion into the dynamic human being so many people have so often complained that he is not. Marr was describing a particular personal experience of seeing Rudd become animated and unguarded, the smooth diplomat's mask removed, transformed from Annabel Crabb's "Ruddbot" into someone recognisable as a fellow creature.

For some reason Marr's observation that anger was Rudd's animating force, "the juice in the machine," drove certain commentators into – ironically enough – a rage. None of the people I saw writing angrily about Marr's diagnosis made the connection between Rudd's anger and their own, which is in itself very telling. It's entirely possible to disagree with parts of the essay while remaining calm, and without rejecting the entire argument or calling it a bad essay: personally I'd argue the toss about whether any single personality trait or emotion could be said to dominate or drive so complex a thing as a personality, and I'd also argue reluctantly, on the basis of decades of personal observation, that a disposition towards anger is at least as much genetic as circumstantial. But neither of those things stood in the way of my reading enjoyment or my appreciation of the quality of the writing and the research.

Those angered by the anger hypothesis, however, seemed to be assuming that this was a savage negative personal criticism of Rudd. But careful reading reveals that this would not have been the case even if the essay had made far more of this conclusion than, in the event, it does. I've heard Marr speak publicly on the subject of anger – in an Adelaide Writers' Week session entitled "Soapbox"; another instance of the way that genre determines content and approach – and my impression then was that he regards it as a profoundly complex, often energising and by no means always, or entirely, "bad" emotion. There's nothing in the essay to suggest that Marr was intending any kind of simple negative judgment, but that was the way commentators chose to take it up.

Given that the essay is an evocative, cleverly structured and thoroughly researched biographical profile of Rudd, working across a broad spectrum of material and sources, it's quite amazing and very dispiriting for anyone interested in a decent standard of public debate that many of its readers should have ignored all but the last four paragraphs. And it's a shame that Kerry O'Brien, interviewing Marr on the 7.30 Report shortly after the essay's publication, also chose to focus on this aspect of it at the expense of the other eighty-four pages.

Thirdly, there's the criticism of Marr's foray into the territory of psychological cause and effect; commentators in the press, on blogs and in the comments section of online newspapers scornfully tossed around such words and phrases as "amateur psychologising," "pop psychology," "psychobabble" and even "armchair psychologist," upon which one bemused blogger had the wit to ask what other kind of psychologist there was.

Many of these criticisms were offered by people apparently so ill-informed that they didn't even know the difference between psychology and psychoanalysis. Others seemed unaware of, or were choosing to ignore, the fact that the obvious connection between childhood experience and the formation of the adult self is one that most of us make frequently as a matter of common sense.

There were two camps here: those who rejected outright any form of psychological or psychoanalytic approach, and those who were accusing Marr of "amateurism" – some of them without noticing, apparently, that their own forays into the realms of journalism were subject to the same accusation. But the essay was positively reviewed online at Inside Story on 8 June by Judith Brett, who said it was "brilliant" and called Marr himself "a fine interpreter of Australian political life." Brett is professor of politics at La Trobe University and is Australia's leading exponent of the use of psychoanalytic concepts and methods in the writing of political history and biography. If she judges that someone else is doing this kind of work well, very few people are in a position to disagree.

Finally, Marr quotes Rudd directly several times on the direct connection between the "mess of his childhood" and his adult motivations and ambitions. Marr isn't just making stuff up. He is, in more than one place, reporting Rudd's own words, as with this telling paragraph from the latter's maiden speech to parliament in 1998:

> When my father was accidentally killed and my mother … was left to rely on the bleak charity of the time … it made a young person think. It made me think that a decent social-security system designed to protect the weak was no bad thing. It made me think that provision of decent public housing to the poor was the right thing to do. When I saw people unnecessarily die in the appallingly under-funded Queensland hospital system … it made me think that

the provision of a decent universal health system should be one of the first responsibilities of the state.

Rudd's father may have died one of these "unnecessary deaths" after the ruptured spleen he sustained in a car accident in 1968 resulted in his death of septicaemia eight weeks later – a death that might perhaps, with better care, have been prevented. Imagine how that possibility could haunt his son. Marr quotes him again, five years later, writing in the *Age* about the now fatherless and temporarily homeless Rudd family sleeping in the car: "People ask: how did I end up in the Labor Party? ... If I trace it back, I just remember sleeping in the car that night and thinking, 'This is crook. This should not have to happen to anyone.'"

It's not Marr who makes these connections. It's Rudd himself. And anyone who rejects the whole idea that childhood experience might shape adult behaviour should at least consider the unfairness of shooting the messenger.

Kerryn Goldsworthy

Judith Brett

Why, after being elected with such high hopes, did Kevin Rudd's star fall so fast? We all know the events: the failure to negotiate the emissions trading scheme through the Senate and the decision to drop the policy until after the next election; the disastrously handled insulation scheme and the lesser disaster of Building the Education Revolution; the decision in an election year to take on one of Australia's most powerful interests, mining, with a new tax. And then there was the increasingly annoying manner, with the repeated tag lines, the priggish, robotic manner. It was only my professional commitment to following Australian politics that stopped me from leaving the room when he appeared yet again in a hard hat and fluoro safety jacket, or sitting in his shirt sleeves beside a hospital bed chatting with studied informality. And if, as the polls indicated, most Australians had switched off too, then his capacity to regain lost ground was very weak. Before he was finally toppled, it was as if he were fading from view before our eyes, still talking, a less and less substantial figure, like the Cheshire cat but with pursed lips and a wagging finger.

The title of David Marr's *Power Trip* points to some answers. Rudd began his maiden speech in federal politics with the words, "Politics is about power." Well, yes and no. Power is complex. It comes in many forms, from coercive power, with its threats and bribes, to the authority to give orders and expect to be obeyed, to the power to persuade people to see a situation as you do and agree with your line of action. And in liberal democracies like Australia, the power of any one political officeholder, even the prime minister, is limited. Marr quotes a shrewd old bureaucrat who has worked with a few prime ministers and wonders if Rudd really understands the way power works at the top: "He isn't afraid to pick a fight, but doesn't then behave like a prime minister: he involves himself so much; puts himself on the line so quickly; doesn't exercise authority by keeping at a distance."

This is the Rudd of "the buck stops with me," who presented himself as the fixer of last resort of all the nation's problems. This is the Rudd who rushed in to take the blame for all the problems of the insulation scheme and whisked his notebook out of his top pocket to note down the names of worried insulators, reassuring them that there would be another phase of government largesse once the problems were sorted out. Why did he think he had to take all the blame? There were a few other candidates – like shonky small-business operators. And no one really expects the prime minister to act as everyone's local member, sorting out each person's problems with this or that government scheme. But having promised something, he then found he couldn't deliver, and he only had himself to blame when he walked away and people were angry. There was failure of judgment here as he promised too much and delivered too little, both in small things like the promise to the insulators and in large policy reversals like the emissions scheme.

Implicit in these failures of judgment is a fantasy of concentration of power in the office of the prime minister. Bucks stop – or not – in many places in liberal parliamentary democracies like ours: in particular with individual ministers, with state premiers and, behind the scenes, with senior public servants. Marr shows convincingly that Rudd is driven by a genuine and deeply held commitment to making Australia a decent place for children to grow up in, a commitment forged in the hard years after his father died. Because his father was a tenant farmer, the family lost its home after he died, and he endured two terrible years as a boarder in a Marist College that instilled in him an icy hatred of the school. Rudd's determination to make Australia a place in which kids didn't have to suffer like he had was accompanied by a determination to re-make himself from a fussy little kid on the margins of other people's lives into someone who was both unassailable and at the centre of things.

But the problem is that, having got there, his hold on power slipped faster than anyone could have imagined. He became, Marr argues, the choke point in the government, just as he was in Goss's government when he ran the Cabinet office. Rudd's micro-management and need to be on top of every detail also had to do with owning all the outcomes of government; he treated senior public servants as underlings, patronised caucus, ignored advice and bypassed his ministers, hogging all the big announcements for himself. And, in the judgment of a former staffer, "His policy positions aren't breakthrough, not particularly new or exciting. After all that work they are dull."

Because he thought power was all about him, he seemed unable to give others the space to be creative, which meant that he couldn't draw on the wisdom of those who are perhaps less clever than he is but have richer life experiences and more understanding of what makes others tick. And he seemed to think that all he had to do was to make announcements. Power is also exercised through persuasion, and here he seemed to have a major blind spot. As we know, he was very sensitive to voters' opinions, but seemed little interested in those of stakeholders. It is mind-boggling that his government decided to introduce a new mining tax without any prior consultation with the industry. Ambushing Australia's most powerful industry in an election year was about as smart as Ben Chifley's taking on the banks. Didn't he remember that the Australian Mining Industry Council's advertising campaign killed the Hawke government's commitment to national land-rights legislation in the 1980s?

The battle with the miners erupted after Marr finished his essay, but it was in character with the man Marr presents, a man for whom power is a brittle exercise in control and who has little understanding of the limits of what one person can do, even when he holds the highest office in the land. Perhaps Rudd will read Marr's essay and learn from it. He does have deep intellectual and emotional reserves. But the concluding scene does not bode well for such an outcome.

Marr and Rudd have been chatting and Rudd asks him about the likely argument of the essay. Marr tells him that he is pursuing the contradictions of his life and wonders aloud if his government will go the way of Goss's. Rudd explodes with controlled fury. It is, says Marr, the most vivid version of Rudd he has yet encountered. "Who is the real Kevin Rudd?" he writes. "He is the man you see when the anger vents. He's a politician with rage at his core, impatient rage." Marr's essay is brilliant: it has all of the sharp observation and unexpected angles, and the lucid, supple prose, that make him such a fine interpreter of Australian political life.

Judith Brett

An earlier version of this piece was published by Inside Story <http://inside.org.au/>.

Brian Howe

David Marr's essay on Kevin Rudd has assumed special importance with the demise of Rudd as prime minister, not only because we can turn to the essay for an understanding of this demise, but also and more importantly for the essay's role as a significant contributor to it. The essay voices the angry disenchantment with Rudd among leading influential political commentators, including Marr himself, Kerry O'Brien of the ABC's *7.30 Report*, and most of the Canberra press gallery.

A feature of this criticism has been its personal nature. Most of Marr's essay is a list of Rudd's sins and the unpleasant aspects of his character. Marr regards Rudd's early life as crucial to understanding him and makes much of Rudd's sensitivity about whether or not the family was made to leave the dairy farm after his father's death and the struggle of his mother to find employment and establish a home. Rudd's early life is significant for Marr, who refers to a psycho-analytic study of British politicians that found those suffering from affection deprivation consequently had an over-developed religious sense. Marr also argues that Rudd in his role as chief of staff played a central role in the defeat of the Goss government in Queensland and that there were similar problems with his prime ministership, including his bureaucratic style as a micromanager, his inability to read people, his "leaden rhetoric" and his obsession with work. Marr quotes with approval columnist Alan Ramsey's assessment of Rudd as "a prissy, precious prick." One wonders how someone with all these unpleasant characteristics was able until early this year to achieve such high ratings as preferred prime minister.

My main interest in David Marr's essay is his concern that as prime minister Rudd had not sought to hide his religious convictions and that, incredibly, they might drive some of his political convictions. He seems surprised that Rudd, while happy to pray with Christians of various persuasions, has liberal views on gays, stem-cell research and the changing patterns of family life. Rudd, like a number of other former or present politicians, reads some theology, would like to see more compassion for boat people and intending asylum seekers, and is deeply committed to improving the quality of life of indigenous people. Rudd also personally asked his caucus to get to know and understand the issue of homelessness, and his government has made the most significant commitment to public housing in the post-war period. The 2020 Summit, which he initiated, did produce one big idea: the National Disability Insurance Scheme that is currently undergoing a feasibility study by a special panel under the auspices of the Productivity Commission.

As Renate Howe has discussed in her recent book on the Australian Student Christian Movement, *A Century of Influence*, there is a long history in this country of people going into politics and public service as an outcome of their religious convictions. Of course, there are many in the parliament who are not driven by religious motives and often the differences are subtle. As well, there are significant differences among Christians, even though we no longer have the sectarian divisions that were historically so important and divisive in Australian politics.

Of course, all politicians have their weaknesses and no doubt Marr identifies some of those in Kevin Rudd. However, when you run through his criticisms, mostly drawn from Rudd's anonymous critics, you have a highly qualified person with academic credentials, who is rather driven, works very hard and expects a lot of those around him, sets high standards for himself and others, is committed to social justice and to delivering a fairer society. It is argued by Marr that Rudd lacked courage, but the fact that Australia escaped the full impact of the global recession owes a great deal to the very strong leadership that he and the rest of the "gang of four" provided at the earliest opportunity. Perhaps he might have done more to ensure that caucus was more involved in policy formation. On the other hand, if people felt strongly enough to destroy his prime ministership, perhaps they might have raised these issues at an earlier stage either in Cabinet or the caucus. It would appear that they did neither.

As I have said, I believe that David Marr's *Quarterly Essay* contributed to Rudd's demise and I also believe that Rudd's *Monthly* essay in October 2006, largely based on the social and ethical ideas of German theologian Dietrich Bonhoeffer, set the framework for his campaign for the prime ministership – an indication that the "chattering classes" are not without their political influence.

Brian Howe

James Boyce

David Marr's analysis of the fuel powering our former prime minister's "power trip" only deepened the mystery concerning his core political values. While anger from childhood experiences is clearly a pillar of his commitment, something more than raw emotion must have provided energy for the gruelling journey to the highest public office in the land. Marr seems aware of this, but having exhausted his search for a motivating value system, opts to return to the familiar theme of the death of the father and the injustice subsequently experienced by mother and son. Fine biographer that he is, Marr seems to miss the significance of the faith journey he so usefully documents and that Rudd described in his landmark 2006 Monthly essay on faith and politics.

Marr was not helped by Rudd's own instinct not to delve too far into a subject that most Australians prefer packaged into the largely meaningless cliché of decency. In the Monthly Rudd sought to identify himself loosely with the socially minded Protestants often called "Christian socialists" who, although not as central to the formation and ideology of the Labor Party in Australia as they were in Britain, still have a long and distinguished record of service to party and nation. Rudd's heroes, Keir Hardie and Andrew Fisher, are political leaders in this mould, but even compared with other new-Labo(u)r Christians such as Kim Beazley or Tony Blair, Kevin Rudd is not easily seen as a modern-day Christian socialist. Nor for that matter can he be pegged as a Catholic activist, historically a more common breed within the ALP. Nevertheless, "Faith in Politics" did provide one helpful clue concerning Rudd's Christian preferences that Marr is not alone in having misread. It says much about the depth of public conversation in Australia that almost four years after Rudd wrote the Monthly essay, and nearly three since he became prime minister, Australians have been told almost nothing of the faith and values of the man Rudd described as "without doubt, the man I admire most in the history of the twentieth century," the German theologian and martyr Dietrich Bonhoeffer.

Dietrich Bonhoeffer is not, as David Marr assumes, an inspiring example of someone "who told the truth to a vicious regime and paid with his life." It is true that during the 1930s Bonhoeffer was a rare voice of resistance within German Protestantism to the Nazi regime, but he was in fact executed for his participation in a plot to assassinate Hitler. Bonhoeffer's move to the centre of power and subversive political action after 1938 as one of a small group of high-ranking conspirators working within German military intelligence was accompanied by a radical journey of faith that was expressed in theological writing of extraordinary imagination and depth.

Both phases of Bonhoeffer's short life were highly productive in literary terms. During the 1930s Bonhoeffer (who, by the way, bore a remarkable physical resemblance to Rudd) wrote a highly influential text, The Cost of Discipleship, which argued that Christians, both individually and collectively through the church, are called to put Christ before all else, including the state. Although this theologically orthodox book is a respected text among conservative Christians, for discerning evangelical readers it poses a potent challenge. It is not difficult to imagine that the uncompromising call to follow Christ wherever he may lead could have provided life-changing inspiration to Rudd as a student leader of the fundamentalist Christian group the Navigators in the 1970s. Here was a book explicitly designed to take orthodox believers beyond the dead-end heresy of the "two kingdoms" (there is one sphere of life which belongs to God and another to worldly powers) and energise them for a life of total discipleship in the world beyond the safety of the church. The quote from this landmark text that Rudd highlighted in the Monthly and perhaps has always remembered – "When Christ calls a man, he bids him come and die" – is explicitly a rejection of the "decent" and "respectable" brand of Christianity to which Australian politicians of all persuasions regularly appeal.

For the socially awkward believer, Bonhoeffer's call to radical discipleship is also reassuringly solitary: "Through the call of Jesus men become individuals ... they are compelled to decide and that decision can only be made by themselves ... Every man is called separately and must follow alone."

This is the call answered by Jim Wallis, Martin Luther King and many an evangelical Christian before and after Kevin Rudd who outgrew the dead work of saving individual souls from "the universal sinfulness of human nature" (still a core Navigators' belief) and instead professed that there was no part of public or private life in which God was not, or should not, be present.

Nevertheless, while the writings of the 1930s Bonhoeffer provide a rallying call to speak and act for the truth whatever the consequences, this theology and life-example has, as Marr points out, limited application to the more complex reality of worldly power. Marr's view that "fascination with Bonhoeffer was odd for a man with Rudd's ambitions" would be correct if Bonhoeffer had been executed in 1938. However, Bonhoeffer's life and work during the last seven years of his life – from 1938 to 1945 – means that he was not "a brave man on the other side ... [who] wasn't dealing with the moral conflicts that inevitably come with government," but rather an agent of German intelligence who knew moral ambiguities that make the ethical challenges of a peacetime Australian prime minister seem tame. As his biographer, former student and friend Eberhard Bethge puts it:

> The year 1932 had put Bonhoeffer into a world where things were comparatively clear-cut, where it was a matter of confessing and denying ... In 1939 he entered the difficult world of assessing what was expedient, of success and failure, of tactics and camouflage. The certainty of his calling in 1932 now changed into the acceptance of the uncertain, the incomplete, and the provisional. The new call demanded quite a different sacrifice, the sacrifice even of a Christian reputation.

Bonhoeffer's new life involved the pursuit of both influence and power, and he drew on extensive personal networks to achieve this. Bethge documents that while before 1938 Bonhoeffer "had been eagerly on the watch for people who could summon up the courage to say No publicly, and were willing to accept dismissal from their posts in consequence," after this time "it was of utmost importance that people of character should remain at the controls in all circumstances and not allow themselves to be displaced."

Once Bonhoeffer became an agent of the military intelligence organisation known as the Abwehr, he participated in necessary shows of loyalty to the Nazi state. The moral conflicts that resulted from his new life were honestly faced in his seminal work Ethics. It is this collection from which Rudd mainly quotes in the Monthly essay. Even after Bonhoeffer was arrested in 1943 (his support for a people-smuggling operation being the main matter of inquiry) and confined in Tegel military prison in Berlin, he was still (once it was known that the military commander of Berlin was a close relative) able to carry on writing. Some letters and about fifty pages of a planned major work of theology were published after the war as *Letters and Papers from Prison*. It was only after the failure of the July 1944 plot to assassinate Hitler and the discovery of secret documents relating to the conspiracy that Bonhoeffer was moved to the notorious Gestapo headquarters and prison in Prinz-Albrecht-Strasse where, needless to say, any opportunity to write disappeared. He was executed, along with Admiral Canaris, General Oster, General Beck, General von Rabenau and others involved in the plot to kill Hitler, at Flossenburg Concentration Camp on 9 April 1945, a month before the war ended. In England Bonhoeffer was soon depicted as a martyr, but much of the German church made (and to some extent still makes) a distinction between believers who were killed by the Nazis for publicly opposing the regime, and those killed for their part in politically conspiring against the state.

In both *Ethics* and *Letters and Papers from Prison*, Bonhoeffer's emphasis was on the necessity for Christians to immerse themselves fully in the reality of the world as it is. In a letter of 21 July 1944 he wrote that:

> I have come to know and understand more and more the profound this-worldliness of Christianity ... For a long time ... I thought I could acquire faith by trying to live a holy life, or something like it. I suppose I wrote *The Cost of Discipleship* as the end of that path ... I discovered later, and I am still discovering right up to this moment, that it is only by living completely in this world that one learns to have faith ... By this-worldliness I mean living unreservedly in life's duties, problems, successes and failures, experiences and perplexities.

Bonhoeffer now embraced secularism as a sign of the world "coming of age." It was Christ who makes possible "true worldliness" and "genuine this-worldliness" – although he noted, in language that his best-known Australian disciple would surely approve, that "I don't mean the shallow and banal this-worldliness of the enlightened, the busy, the comfortable, or the lascivious, but the profound this-worldliness characterised by discipline and the constant knowledge of death and resurrection."

If "Christ is no longer an object of religion, but something quite different, really the Lord of the world ... what [asked Bonhoeffer] does that mean?" This question would have an individual answer for every follower of Christ but seems to embrace political ambition as a vital expression of the Christian mission.

Rudd's *Monthly* essay was largely a manifesto for opposition, not power. It gave no sense of Bonhoeffer's later theological or life journey, and only a few clues as to how the prime minister's own "power trip" might relate to this. It was in fact quite a peculiar essay (that cries out for a sequel!). While the subject was supposedly "faith in politics," almost the only subject explored is the responsibility of the church to speak its truth on public-policy matters from *outside* the realms of power. Rudd's purpose seemed to be two-fold: to challenge the association of Christians with conservative politics, and to give both party and nation a sense that this aspiring leader was a values-driven man belonging to a Christian tradition we could all (even the largely secular Labor caucus) understand. The achievement of these objectives meant staying with the orthodox 1930s Bonhoeffer and presenting a somewhat misleading view of his hero as a preacher of the social gospel who "died a Christian pastor, committed social democrat and passionate internationalist."

In fact, Bonhoeffer no more easily fits into a party-political or Christian socialist tradition than does Rudd himself. This is not a question of contradiction – with sufficient effort the buttons can be just about done up, even though the clothing was made for others – but the attire is never comfortable. What needs to be remembered is that Rudd's carefully packaged public portrayal is unlikely to be a full summation either of his understanding of Bonhoeffer or of the impact the German martyr's life and writings had on his own life. Rudd has undoubtedly read *Ethics* and *Letters and Papers from Prison*. It is surely highly probable that these mature works, which deal with the moral challenges consequent to full immersion in the world as it is, have been an important influence on him. A further clue that this is the case is provided by Rudd's recurring description of issues like climate change and asylum seekers as the great moral challenges "*of our age.*" For the early Bonhoeffer, the responsibility of the church and individual Christians is largely timeless, but in his mature work the emphasis is on the here and now, the ethical challenge of the new secular world or what he calls "*this age*" – "What is true for always is precisely not true for 'today.'"

Does it change anything that Dietrich Bonhoeffer might have been more relevant to Rudd's political journey than David Marr assumes? Are we still not left with the fact that Rudd's decision to defer the emissions trading scheme until 2012 was, as Tim Flannery has recently put it, "a funk in the true sense of the word: a shirking of responsibility," and that his approach to asylum seekers, another self-described "great challenge of our age," stands in horrible contradiction to the "biblical injunction to care for the stranger in our midst"? After all, doesn't Bonhoeffer himself (as Rudd pointed out) make clear that obedience to God's will is not an ethical response "until it issues in actions that can be socially valued"?

Perhaps his detractors are right, and even if Rudd holds deep moral convictions, he lacked the courage to act on them. However, as the mining-tax furore suggests, there can be no certainty on this question. The final enigma of Kevin Rudd's prime ministership is that we may never know if Rudd's sacking was more associated with a determination to defend his principles or a readiness to abandon them. If he becomes a senior minister again, the man himself may yet provide the answer. Moreover, if the Rudd power trip is to continue, our former leader would do well to use the break in his journey to listen once more to his hero. He might begin with a piece Bonhoeffer wrote as a Christmas present for his co-conspirators at the end of the terrible year of 1942, a reflection which seems oddly relevant to a former prime minister facing a party and nation that no longer know what, if anything, he believes in:

> Are we still of any use? We have been silent witnesses of evil deeds; we have been drenched by many storms; we have learnt the arts of equivocation and pretence; experience has made us suspicious of others and kept us from being truthful and open; intolerable conflicts have worn us down and even made us cynical. Are we still of any use? … Will our inward power of resistance be strong enough, and our honesty with ourselves remorseless enough for us to find our way back to simplicity and straightforwardness?

Kevin Rudd's faith seems to have been the most quirky of any Australian prime minister since Alfred Deakin, and it surely remains the wild card in his political career. Could our policy-junkie former leader, finally bereft of his army of advisers and bureaucrats, use his involuntary holiday to, like Deakin before him, converse with the spirits of the dead? My hope is that, freed from the straightjacket of prime ministerial ambition, Kevin Rudd might yet provide true moral leadership on the most pressing issues of our age. Eberhard Bethge believed that Dietrich Bonhoeffer "possessed in a high degree the capacity to help other people to come to a decision"; so perhaps we should all be praying that Rudd remains enough of a Catholic to believe in the value of talking with saints.

James Boyce

David Marr

"Wow! Just as well your essay sold well early!" The message arrived as I was walking into a conference on Patrick White in London. Christ, I thought, are we being sued? Has it been withdrawn?

"What's happening?" I asked.

Fran Kelly replied a few minutes later: "Nothing yet – Julia still in Rudd's office – Sky quotes the right has shifted against KR. He's stuffed."

I began to write QE38 when Rudd was still travelling well in the polls. The collapse of his figures was the sad background music of the project. But I didn't see his end coming. Annabel Crabb lived in terror that Malcolm Turnbull might be "on the scrapheap" before her *Quarterly Essay* was done. I was – along with just about everyone I spoke to at the time in the press gallery and the Labor Party – confident Rudd would hold on. In the end, Turnbull outlived QE34 by seven months; Kevin Rudd survived QE38 by only three weeks.

My foolhardy assertion that talk of rolling Rudd before the elections was "rubbish" remains to protect me from those who say I have his blood on my hands. Intervention was all I wished on the prime minister. Not execution. In the end his colleagues were too angry or too gutless to demand change. Instead they tore him down. The British were agog at the surgical despatch of a struggling Labor leader only months before the polls. That's the fate so many had wished on Gordon Brown. Labor was praised in London for the daring, the professionalism, the hard-headed approach to party survival that Labour had failed to display. As this reply goes to press, the wisdom of Rudd's execution is, to put it mildly, in question. By the first week of August the polls were as bad for Labor under Julia Gillard as they were at their worst for Rudd. As to the outcome: I make no prediction.

Power Trip has been generously received and Rudd's fall has allowed many to speak on the record of the problems I identified in the man and his management of power. Some of this wonderful new material emerges in the correspondence to this essay. More is emerging all the time. I'm confident my picture of Rudd will survive the new, and welcome, spirit of indiscretion sweeping the nation.

Two responses to *Power Trip* surprised me. At a do in a Sydney bookshop a few days after publication, Alison Broinowski reproached me for feeding into the anti-Rudd agenda of News Limited. This sophisticated woman was not alone in arguing that I owed some sort of higher obligation to protect the man. I was letting down the side. I should shut up. Sylvia Lawson blogged: "Whatever the eventual profit may be in an analysis of Kevin Rudd's personality, now is not the time for it … Any liberal, or left-liberal, writer's overriding present projects should work, openly or otherwise, on the side of social democracy." *Quarterly Essay* readers don't need the long answer. The short is this: rubbish.

My anger management worked perfectly, up to a point. Even as the prime minister was raging at me on the terrace of that Mackay hotel, I knew I would end the essay with this sighting of the Real Rudd in action. "Who is this man?" is the fundamental question of the essay. From his life and writing, I offered many answers. But here on the last page – making sense, I hoped, of many mysteries of this complicated figure – I placed the notion that he is driven by anger, even rage. The idea certainly grabbed attention. Nothing in the essay had such an impact or was quoted so often as the line: "It's the juice in the machine."

Anger can drive fine ambitions. Anger doesn't disqualify a man from high office. But any reading of his career shows the control of anger is an issue with Rudd. His rage at the hapless RAAF stewardess who brought him the wrong meal marked him down sharply in the public's estimation – an incident I thought so familiar it need not be revisited in the essay. Nothing since has shaken my conviction that anger fuels Rudd's ambitions – perhaps more, now, than ever before.

Failing to persuade every last one of my readers about the role of anger in Rudd's life did not surprise me. What I found surprising was the notion that I shouldn't have tried to dig deeply into Rudd's character. "You have taken my patch," declared psychiatry professor Jayashri Kulkarni on *Q&A*. "I find it incredibly offensive that you have dared to do something which we take such great pains to do … I really don't think that you are qualified to do this."

I relied primarily on the man's own accounts of how life has shaped him. We talked. He answered intrusive questions. I interrogated witnesses, tracked down documents and watched him in action. All the usual things. I measured his early years against familiar patterns in the lives of political leaders in the US and the UK. I noted where he did and didn't fit this strange template of loss and determination. What I didn't try was amateur psychiatry. I'm a long-time critic of the Freudian or Jungian biography. They strike me as bogus: applying clinical theory to subjects the author has not examined on the couch. So I used neither the theories nor the language of psychiatry. That took, I must say, heroic restraint. Google "narcissism" and watch Dr Freud's explanation for the peculiarities of leaders like Kevin Rudd – their greatness and weakness – roll out before your eyes.

To be in Britain at the time of Rudd's fall was bizarre. Chattering on the BBC and writing for Fairfax meant I didn't attend much of the White conference. Thank heavens, I found the time for Dr Jaroslav Kusnír's absorbing paper on "The Critical Reception of Patrick White's Fiction in Slovakia and the Czech Republic." (Little or none, it seems.) One afternoon of wretched hayfever in the gardens at Sissinghurst, half a dozen Australians sat in the Lime Walk – or was it the Moat Walk? – talking Rudd and his downfall. We were a bunch of strangers who had all left home before it happened, meeting by accident on the far side of the world to ask the question that still has not been answered: why?

We know he was essentially friendless in caucus. We know Labor's sense of obligation to the man who brought the party in from the wilderness had evaporated. Narratives have already appeared telling who moved when to bring him down. Yet the deeper question of the party's motive remains to be explored. Nothing has so intrigued me about Rudd as his peculiar behaviour on the night he won office: his odd attitude to victory, his inwardness, his strange lack of rapport with a crowd begging him to celebrate. His fall made me think about that night again and how victory seemed to Rudd to be so much about Rudd. My sense is that from first to last, Rudd exercised power – the power he had craved for so long – not as the leader of his party or the head of government. He exercised power as if it were his own. The failings that have been held against him – the passion for control, the offhand dealings with Cabinet, the caucus and the public service – were only symptoms of this. Rudd saw power as a personal possession. The mistake was fundamental. Even if his bond with the Australian people had not frayed so badly, the situation would have become intolerable. In late June, in order to restore the normal order of things, the party bosses brought Kevin Rudd's power trip to an end.

David Marr

James Boyce is the author of *Van Diemen's Land* and the forthcoming *1835*, as well as the Tasmania chapter of *First Australians*, the companion book to the SBS TV series. He is an honorary research associate at the University of Tasmania's Centre for Environmental Studies.

Judith Brett is the author of *Quarterly Essay 19, Relaxed and Comfortable* and *Quarterly Essay 29, Exit Right*, as well as the books *Robert Menzies' Forgotten People* and *Australian Liberals and the Moral Middle Class*. She is a professor of politics at La Trobe University.

Annabel Crabb's latest book is *Rise of the Ruddbot*. She is the author of *Quarterly Essay 34, Stop at Nothing*, and the ABC's chief online political writer.

Kerryn Goldsworthy taught literature at the University of Melbourne for almost twenty years. A former editor of *Australian Book Review*, she has edited four anthologies of Australian writing. She blogs at <www.stilllifewithcat.blogspot.com>.

Brian Howe was the deputy prime minister and minister for health, housing and community services in the Keating government.

David Marr is the author of *Patrick White: A Life* and *Quarterly Essay 26, His Master's Voice*, and co-author with Marian Wilkinson of *Dark Victory*. He has written for the *Bulletin* and the *Sydney Morning Herald* and has been editor of the *National Times*, a reporter for *Four Corners* and presenter of ABC TV's *Media Watch*.

Laura Tingle is the political editor of the *Australian Financial Review*.

Chris Uhlmann is the political editor of ABC News 24. Previously, from August 2009 until April 2010, he was the political editor of the *7.30 Report*.

Hugh White is a professor of strategic studies at ANU and a visiting fellow at the Lowy Institute. He has been an intelligence analyst with the Office of National Assessments, a journalist with the *Sydney Morning Herald*, a senior adviser to Defence Minister Kim Beazley and Prime Minister Bob Hawke, and a senior official in the Department of Defence, where from 1995 to 2000 he was deputy secretary for strategy and intelligence and a co-author of Australia's Defence White Paper 2000.

SUBSCRIBE to Quarterly Essay & SAVE nearly 40% off the cover price

Subscriptions: Receive a discount and never miss an issue. Mailed direct to your door.
- ☐ **1 year subscription** (4 issues): $49 a year within Australia incl. GST. Outside Australia $79.
- ☐ **2 year subscription** (8 issues): $95 a year within Australia incl. GST. Outside Australia $155.
- * All prices include postage and handling.

Back Issues: (Prices include postage and handling.)

- ☐ **QE 1** ($10.95) Robert Manne *In Denial*
- ☐ **QE 2** ($10.95) John Birmingham *Appeasing Jakarta*
- ☐ **QE 4** ($10.95) Don Watson *Rabbit Syndrome*
- ☐ **QE 5** ($12.95) Mungo MacCallum *Girt by Sea*
- ☐ **QE 6** ($12.95) John Button *Beyond Belief*
- ☐ **QE 7** ($12.95) John Martinkus *Paradise Betrayed*
- ☐ **QE 8** ($12.95) Amanda Lohrey *Groundswell*
- ☐ **QE 10** ($13.95) Gideon Haigh *Bad Company*
- ☐ **QE 11** ($13.95) Germaine Greer *Whitefella Jump Up*
- ☐ **QE 12** ($13.95) David Malouf *Made in England*
- ☐ **QE 13** ($13.95) Robert Manne with David Corlett *Sending Them Home*
- ☐ **QE 14** ($14.95) Paul McGeough *Mission Impossible*
- ☐ **QE 15** ($14.95) Margaret Simons *Latham's World*
- ☐ **QE 16** ($14.95) Raimond Gaita *Breach of Trust*
- ☐ **QE 17** ($14.95) John Hirst *"Kangaroo Court"*
- ☐ **QE 18** ($14.95) Gail Bell *The Worried Well*
- ☐ **QE 19** ($15.95) Judith Brett *Relaxed & Comfortable*
- ☐ **QE 20** ($15.95) John Birmingham *A Time for War*
- ☐ **QE 21** ($15.95) Clive Hamilton *What's Left?*
- ☐ **QE 22** ($15.95) Amanda Lohrey *Voting for Jesus*
- ☐ **QE 23** ($15.95) Inga Clendinnen *The History Question*
- ☐ **QE 24** ($15.95) Robyn Davidson *No Fixed Address*
- ☐ **QE 25** ($15.95) Peter Hartcher *Bipolar Nation*
- ☐ **QE 26** ($15.95) David Marr *His Master's Voice*
- ☐ **QE 27** ($15.95) Ian Lowe *Reaction Time*
- ☐ **QE 28** ($15.95) Judith Brett *Exit Right*
- ☐ **QE 29** ($16.95) Anne Manne *Love & Money*
- ☐ **QE 30** ($16.95) Paul Toohey *Last Drinks*
- ☐ **QE 31** ($16.95) Tim Flannery *Now or Never*
- ☐ **QE 32** ($16.95) Kate Jennings *American Revolution*
- ☐ **QE 33** ($17.95) Guy Pearse *Quarry Vision*
- ☐ **QE 34** ($17.95) Annabel Crabb *Stop at Nothing*
- ☐ **QE 35** ($17.95) Noel Pearson *Radical Hope*
- ☐ **QE 36** ($17.95) Mungo MacCallum *Australian Story*
- ☐ **QE 37** ($20.95) Waleed Aly *What's Right?*
- ☐ **QE 38** ($20.95) David Marr *Power Trip*

Payment Details: I enclose a cheque/money order made out to Schwartz Media Pty Ltd. Please debit my credit card (Mastercard or Visa accepted).

Card No. ☐☐☐☐ ☐☐☐☐ ☐☐☐☐ ☐☐☐☐

Expiry date   /   Amount $

Cardholder's name   Signature

Name

Address

Email

Post or fax this form to: Quarterly Essay, Reply Paid 79448, Melbourne VIC 3000 / Tel: (03) 9486 0288 / Fax: (03) 9486 0244 / Email: subscribe@blackincbooks.com

Subscribe online at **www.quarterlyessay.com**